T5-AFN-104

Decision Making and Planning for the Corporate Treasurer

–Decision Making and Planning for the Corporate Treasurer–

HAROLD BIERMAN, Jr.

The Nicholas H. Noyes Professor of Business Administration
Graduate School of Business and Public Administration
Cornell University

with verse contributions by

Florence M. Kelso

A Wiley-Interscience Publication

JOHN WILEY & SONS, New York • London • Sydney • Toronto

658.15
B5879

166364

Copyright © 1977 by John Wiley & Sons, Inc.

All rights reserved. Published simultaneously in Canada.

No part of this book may be reproduced by any means,
nor transmitted, nor translated into a machine language
without the written permission of the publisher.

Library of Congress Cataloging in Publication Data
Bierman, Harold.
  Decision making and planning for the corporate treasurer.

  (Wiley series on systems and controls for financial management)
  "A Wiley-Interscience publication."
  Includes index.
  1. Corporations—Finance. I. Title.

HG4011.B46   658.1'5   76-58435
ISBN 0-471-07238-9

Printed in the United States of America

10 9 8 7 6 5 4 3 2 1

SERIES PREFACE

No one needs to tell the reader that the world is changing. He sees it all too clearly. The immutable, the constant, the unchanging of a decade or two ago no longer represent the latest thinking—on *any* subject, whether morals, medicine, politics, economics, or religion. Change has always been with us, but the pace has been accelerating, especially in the postwar years.

Business, particularly with the advent of the electronic computer some 20 years ago, has also undergone change. New disciplines have sprung up. New professions are born. New skills are in demand. And the need is ever greater to blend the new skills with those of the older professions to meet the demands of modern business.

The accounting and financial functions certainly are no exception. The constancy of change is as pervasive in these fields as it is in any other. Industry is moving toward an integration of many of the information gathering, processing, and analyzing functions under the impetus of the so-called systems approach. Such corporate territory has been, tradition-ally, the responsibility of the accountant and the financial man. It still is, to a large extent—but times are changing.

Does this, then, spell the early demise of the accountant as we know him today? Does it augur a lessening of influence for the financial specialists in today's corporate hierarchy? We think not. We maintain, however, that it is incumbent upon today's accountant and today's financial man to learn *today's* thinking and to *use today's* skills. It is for this reason the Wiley Series on Systems and Controls for Financial Management is being developed.

Recognizing the broad spectrum of interests and activities that the series title encompasses, we plan a number of volumes, each representing the latest thinking, written by a recognized authority, on a particular facet of the financial man's responsibilities. The subjects contemplated for discussion within the series range from production accounting systems to planning, to corporate records, to control of cash. Each book is an in-depth study of one subject within this group. Each is intended to be a practical, working tool for the businessman in general and the financial man and accountant in particular.

ROBERT L. SHULTIS
FRANK M. MASTROMANO

PREFACE

Financial planning, which this book defines,
Will increase the profits from assembly lines.

In the past twenty-five years there has been a knowledge explosion in the areas of managerial finance and investment decision making. The literature on business decision making has shifted from a more or less intuitive qualitative approach to one that is much more analytical and mathematical. Taking the period since 1952, some of the more significant publishing milestones of interest are the following:

1952   Dean, Joel, *Capital Budgeting* (New York: Columbia University Press, 1951).

1958   Hirshleifer, Jack, "On the Theory of Optimal Investment Decision," *Journal of Political Economy,* August.

1958   Modigliani, F. and M. H. Miller, "The Cost of Capital, Corporate Finance, and the Theory of Investment," *American Economic Review,* June.

1959   Markowitz, H. M., *Portfolio Selection: Efficient Diversification of Investment* (New York: Cowles Foundation Monograph No. 16).

1964   Sharpe, W. F., "Capital Asset Prices: A Theory of Market Equilibrium under Conditions of Risk," *Journal of Finance,* September.

1971   Fama, E. and M. H. Miller, *The Theory of Finance* (New York: Holt, Rinehart and Winston).

The 24-year-old students graduating with their MBAs in 1952 will be 49 years old in 1977. Unless they have continued their finance education, formally or informally, they will have missed a series of developments that affect practical corporate financial decision making in a myriad of ways.

Many of the writings cited above are of a quantitative nature. Modern finance has become more and more quantitative, with a result that a large portion of the current literature is not readily understandable to a large percentage of the managerial community.

An analytical approach to financial decisions is useful for two important reasons:

1. The use of analysis (including a mathematical model) may give a specific optimum answer.
2. The use of the model may lead to a better understanding of the decision process, which in turn may lead to a better decision, even where it is not possible to apply the model and obtain a specific answer.

This book attempts to interpret the current state of the art in investment and financial decision making as it applies to the corporate treasurer's position and to make clear how the theories developed in academia can be used to better manage business firms.

Mathematical models of financial decisions do not replace judgment, but rather apply the judgment and experience of the decision maker more effectively to the problem studied. Many of the situations with which we deal are decisions made under uncertainty; thus the decision indicated by the model may, after the event has occurred, turn out to be a less desirable alternative than others that were available. This is, of course, a characteristic of decision making under uncertainty. When there is uncertainty there is generally a probability that an event may occur for which there is a better action than the action chosen.

Rather than clutter the pages of this book with mathematical proofs that have been developed elsewhere, an attempt has been made to interpret the models and make clear their uses and limitations. Some algebra, symbols, and graphs are used. However, all that is required is a little patience with basic mathematics. No understanding of advanced mathematics is required. The mathematical models generally have been translated into words and supplemented by numerical examples to ensure that the basic principles are understood.

Simplifying assumptions have been made in many places. The reader must evaluate the extent of damage done to the usefulness of each model by the assumptions that are the basis of the model. All model building involves abstracting from the complexities of the real world.

Imagine what would happen if managers tried to incorporate all the consequences of each of their decisions every time they make decisions. Generally, managers focus on the more immediate and apparent consequences of their actions, rather than those which are far removed and difficult to determine. Sometimes this has severe repercussions, as when they neglect externalities associated with the firm's actions. For example, a manager dumping pollutants in a stream is considering only the immediate consequences. If it is thought to be desirable that downstream effects are incorporated also, then this consideration must be built into the system (the motivation may be supplied by government action).

If this book is successful, the reader will continue the search for better ways of analyzing financial decisions. It is a characteristic of written material in the area of finance that it becomes obsolete shortly after publication. This is a price we pay for progress. A safe prediction is that one can expect to see more and more analysis (similar to that presented in this book) in the area of managerial finance.

Thanks are expressed to Sy Smidt and Jerry Hass who have helped me learn finance. They are very valuable colleagues.

I also express my great appreciation to Florence M. Kelso for permission to publish the rhymes that introduce each chapter. She suggests that

> *You could do worse*
> *Than just read the verse.*

HAROLD BIERMAN, JR.

Ithaca, New York
November 1976

CONTENTS

Chapter 1

CORPORATE FINANCIAL PLANNING

You must know the right figure. This may sound pedantic,
But it helps make good decisions, both business and romantic.

The essentials of corporate financial planning can be summarized by the following four questions:

1. What kind of financing is desirable and when?
2. How should the cash and other assets that have been acquired be used?
3. How and when should funds be returned to investors?
4. What corporate strategy should be followed relative to growth through product diversification, mergers and acquisitions?

First and most importantly, there are no simple answers to any of the questions. This book attempts to develop some generalizations that will lead to improved financial decision making. There are some situations for which the alternatives may be listed, and we can conclude that one alternative is the best. In other situations, in order to analyze the situation, it is necessary to make simplifying assumptions, and we are less sure that the solution holds for real world conditions. One of the most famous and respected finance articles ever published proved that under given conditions the value of a firm was not affected by its capital structure.[1] From that article has flowed an avalanche of useful insights, but a primary conclusion of the paper was not valid in a real

---

[1]F. Modigliani and M.H. Miller, "The Cost of Capital, Corporate Finance and the Theory of Investment," *American Economic Review,* June 1958.

world in which there are income taxes. With income taxes (or with market imperfections) it is now agreed that capital structure decisions do affect the value of a firm. Nevertheless, studying the no tax situation was extremely important because it helped us to isolate the relevant and nonrelevant factors.

The term corporate financial planning correctly implies that future consequences are considered in making decisions today. Too frequently top managers place one consideration ahead of all others. What will be the immediate effect of the decision on the firm's stock price? This consideration can take several forms, such as concern for the effect on *today's* return on investment, income, and earnings per share. Although the same managers will indicate that they also consider the long-run effects, it is not always possible to do so on an ad hoc basis.

It is argued in this book that improvements in financial decision making will lead to opportunities for improving the wealth position of stockholders. Answers to the four questions are offered. Unfortunately, many of the exact answers require qualification. The person who requires well-defined exact answers to all questions should not be making decisions in the area of corporate financial planning.

Corporate financial planning also implies that an objective or goal has been set. Throughout the book the appropriateness of different goals is evaluated.

One hears discussions of a variety of objectives for a firm, such as maximization of:

Sales
Share of market
Profits or earnings per share
Return on investment
Growth
Stock price

Unfortunately, each of these objectives is deficient in some sense as a guide for managerial action. Although increased sales are good if they lead to increased profits, increased sales (or market share) are not desirable if the sales are "bought" by decreasing profits. Increased profits are good, but not if the amount of investment necessary to accomplish the increase could have been put to better use by the investor, or if the effect on immediate earnings per share growth is positive, but in the long run would result in a lower growth rate of earnings. Maintaining a high return on investment (ROI) may be desirable, but not if it is accomplished by rejecting desirable investments that will raise total net income; more on this later. Although "maximization of the stockholders' well being" is somewhat ambiguous and requires further explanation, it comes closest to being the appropriate guide for managerial action.

But what decisions lead to a maximization of stockholders' well being? The diversity of opinion regarding what constitutes good financial planning is exemplified by a well-known company that has gone completely contrary to conventional financial wisdom during the period of 1947 to the present. It is essentially a one-product firm that has spurned the merger movement of the 1960s. As of the end of 1974, it had an unusually high current ratio (ratio of current assets to current liabilities) of 4.2. It had zero long-term debt despite the presence of stockholders equity of $637 million, and minimum earnings for the previous five years of $28 million. Although it does some small amount of borrowing from foreign banks ($9 million as of 1974), it had zero domestic bank debt. The name of the company is Polaroid.

DECISION MAKING AND FINANCIAL DECISIONS

It comes as no surprise that man makes decisions and that many financial executives make good decisions without the aid of books and courses of study in decision making. Why study the subject of financial decision making? In fact, why study any subject? You should remember that long ago there was an ancestor of yours, with a native intelligence that matched yours, who did not know of the wheel. That which is a brilliant innovation, a result of rare genius, becomes available to great numbers of lesser intellects through the interpretative mediums of books and teachers. Hopefully by studying financial decision making we can increase the likelihood of making "good" decisions. We can improve decision making by improving our general understanding and approach to the decision process and by improving our techniques for approaching specific decisions.

We want to have a decision process that is "most effective" and likely to lead to decisions that are consistent with the goals of the organization. Why do we not choose *the* correct decision? Given a suitably powerful forecasting device (always correct in its prognostications), we could make many more correct decisions. Unfortunately, our ability to forecast the future is very limited. Ford Motor Company would not have produced the Edsel if it could have predicted the demand (market surveys were misleading). Lockheed management would not have authorized bribe payments if it could have forecast their consequences (or if they had decided to stand or fall based on ethical actions).

This book is oriented to business firms organized to make profits. However, to describe the primary goal of any business corporation as the maximization of profits is to simplify excessively. The measure of profits presented to the managers and stockholders is generally a very inadequate measure of the change in well-being of the corporation, and if the goal is to maximize this measure the stockholders are apt to be short-changed. For example, the conventional accounting measure of income omits the opportunity cost of the funds utilized in an investment. The measure of profits might be increasing through time and the stockholders' position improving, but their position might increase even more if the earnings were distributed to them and they were able to invest the funds outside the firm.

The financial accountant is a scorekeeper. He reports on where the firm is now and how it has performed through time. In a manner similar to that of athletic games, the method of scoring a firm's operations affects how the business game is played. To understand why decisions are made, it is necessary to understand how a decision will affect the well-being of the decision maker. If a desirable decision from the stockholders' viewpoint will adversely affect income as measured by the accountant, a factor has been introduced that amounts to a conflict of interest. Although such devices as stock option plans have been used to minimize this conflict, it still exists in many instances.

Businessmen have been putting numbers together for the purposes of decision making for centuries. Although we can agree that quantitative approaches to decision making are not a recent discovery, it is also true that several developments have accelerated the rate of usage of quantitative methods. For example, consider the advent of the electronic computer, the entry of mathematically trained technicians into business decision making, resulting in the development of such optimization techniques as mathematical programming, inventory and queueing models, and the splitting off from classical statistics of a body of knowledge called modern statistical decision theory. The list could be made much longer, but the above give an indication of why many would say there has been a revolution in the art of decision making in recent years.

Decisions may be classified in numerous ways. First let us consider the frequency of the decision, and divide decisions into two classifications:

1. A unique one-time decision
2. A repetitive decision with either reasonably constant or randomly spaced time between decisions

Most unique one-shot decisions are convertible into randomly spaced decisions; however, it is still true that there are many decisions that are unique. They may be repeated, but there is likely to be a large space of time between decisions. A firm may choose a plant site or a new executive vice-president. Those are important decisions, and despite the fact that we may make the decision only once for this particular plant and vice-presidency, we may choose to spend considerable time and effort in making the decisions because of their importance.

Many decisions are repetitive, and fortunately the store of information we gather for making the previous decisions may be carried forward and applied to the decisions coming up. Complex decisions become routine through familiarity. A New Yorker of average intelligence can choose the correct subway in New York City; visitors of superior intelligence are apt to head off in the wrong direction, especially if they read the maps or ask directions. The computation of the net present value of an investment and the application of a simple accept or reject decision rule is a complex task for managers the first time they approach the problem. After the fiftieth computation an adventuresome clerk is likely to complain of the routine work load (if one complains sufficiently, the task may be given to a computer).

It is very helpful when we can move a decision from the unique classification to the repetitive classification, for then there is a possibility that we can effectively use information accumulated for similar decisions made in the past. Hopefully we can routinize the decision. However not all repetitive decisions can be made routine. Repetitive decisions may be classified as to whether or not each decision is unique in some manner. We can imagine a continuous spectrum measuring the different degrees of uniqueness of decisions. The subway decision for the New Yorker going to work is an example of a relatively homogeneous set of repetitive decisions (assuming no special trips requiring special travel plans). A financial executive establishing decision rules for issuing bonds is faced with this same type of repetitive decision.

On the other hand, there are many decisions that although repetitive, are each a little (or greatly) different from previous decisions. The hiring of personnel for managerial jobs or promoting individuals are examples of repetitive but different decisions.

Decisions may also be classified as to the degree of importance of the outcome. If the future existence of the firm hinges on the outcome of the decision, this decision will receive a different degree of consideration than if the decision is apt to affect the level of profit by some small amount.

Fortunately for our mental health, most decisions we make are not of crucial importance; that is, no matter how the decisions turn out, the organization will survive and the decision maker will survive also.

Placing the decision in perspective is extremely important. Taking a broad point of view, how important is the decision? Is it worthy of the effort being devoted to its resolution? In technical language, what is the value of additional information and how does the value compare with the cost of obtaining the information?

There are other important characteristics of decision making. We may make an incorrect decision and have it turn out to be correct, that is, we can make a correct decision for the wrong reasons. We may decide incorrectly not to promote Mr. Jones, who then moves on to a better job, and replace him with a person who turns out to be outstanding. Because of random events, a well-made and well-researched decision may turn out to be incorrect, or an "incorrect" decision may turn out to be correct. Whenever we deal with decision making under uncertainty, we face the possibility of a "bad" outcome in spite of a correct a priori decision.

In evaluating a business plan (a course of action or a set of decisions that have long-run implications where these implications have been considered) before the plan has been implemented, we want to determine whether or not the plan has considered all factors and has effectively brought them into the analysis. After the plans have been executed and we are attempting to evaluate management's performance, it is important to consider the information available to management at the time of setting the plan rather than the information currently available. In the fall of 1973 it was not difficult to see that there was an oil shortage. Was it as easy to see that shortage in the spring of 1973? Today would you say that the planning for energy contingencies had advanced significantly since 1973?

An outstanding management might have anticipated the types of events that occurred in 1973, but it is not shocking if the events were not perfectly anticipated. A mediocre management is likely to be critical in retrospect of others who failed to anticipate the obvious (after the fact). But the crucial question will always be, what do we do now, where we do not yet know what is going to happen in the future?

In the next chapter we apply the basic decision techniques to financial decisions. We see that defining the elements of decision making enables us to grasp better the critical factors that distinguish the consequences of one action compared to another.

FINANCIAL PLANNING

Financial planning is frequently defined as forecasting the amount of cash that will be needed, or will be generated, in the coming time periods. More sophisticated planning systems develop a complete set of financial reports for each set of decisions considered.

This type of pro forma accounting is important to a finance officer, but is not the topic of discussion of this book. We assume that if the consequences of a decision can be forecasted, a set of financial statements can be prepared (by hand or by computer) that reflects the consequences of the decision.

The focus of this book is the formulation of financial policy and plans so that the results, based on the given set of assumptions, will tend to maximize the well-being of the investors.

The reader may well wonder what is the difference between financial planning and financial decision making. The distinction is not clear cut, and it would not be useful for us to pretend that it is. However, we use the term planning in the title of this book because we are concerned with decisions that affect future operations and profits. We are concerned with establishing financial policy so that there are guidelines for future decisions. In a sense, the term "decision" implies a short-sightedness that is eliminated by the term "planning."

CHAPTER 2

WORKING CAPITAL DECISIONS

"Take the cash and let the credit go"*
Omar wisely said.
Borrow cash and let the credit flow—
Alas, poor Grant is dead.

Provided with enough information, the management scientists can solve the problems of the optimum amount of cash, the optimum credit policy, and the optimum inventory amount. When they complete this analysis, unless they then consider the optimum amount of working capital (not just the algebraic sum of optimum cash, accounts receivable, and inventories), they have stopped short of solving the interesting and relevant problem. It is necessary for the financial planner to interrelate the several decisions rather than stopping after solving subcomponents. We first discuss the different subcomponents and then consider the implications of the decisions to the overall firm.

There are two functions served by working capital. One is the working asset function. It is relatively easy to recommend policies for this function. The second function is a safety function (a buffer against bad events), and this leads to a problem that is much more difficult to solve.

Let us consider a company that in 1973 had sales of $1.6 billion and earnings of $35 million. In 1974 the firm had $1.8 billion of sales and net earnings of $11 million. In 1975 the firm was heading for bankruptcy, and by February 1976 it was bankrupt. What caused the W.T. Grant Company bankruptcy?

In 1973 the W.T. Grant Company announced a change in its credit

---

*"The Rubaiyat of Omar Khayyam" Edward Fitzgerald, Stanza 1; in *Familiar Quotations,* John Bartlett, Little, Brown and Company, Boston, 1955, p. 531.

policy. In the 52-week period ending January 30, 1975, the company incurred gross credit expenses of $249 million, including a provision for doubtful accounts for $156 million (the previous year the provision was $21 million). The change in credit policy was probably not the only factor contributing to the financial difficulties (an expansion of the product line and a change in store image also contributed), but it certainly triggered a reaction in the minds of the company's creditors that led to disaster.

DECISIONS INVOLVING CASH AND SECURITIES

Decisions in the administration of cash and short-term securities are not susceptible to simple rules or answers. Part of the difficulty stems from the risk attitudes of the treasurer and other officers about the possibility of a shortage of cash. To some extent the corporation has bought peace of mind for its treasurer when it has paid $150,000 during a year for a $20,000,000 credit agreement that it has not used. To an outside observer this may seem to be a high price to pay for insurance against risk, but to management the elimination of one type of financial risk may be worth $150,000, because it enables them to assume risks in other areas.

This section describes decisions that could be made in the management of cash and near-cash resources and possible methods of analysis for making these decisions. The analysis is not a prescription leading to perfect decisions about cash and short-term securities. Rather it is an attempt to point up some of the relevant considerations and methods of incorporating these considerations into the decision process.

The basic decisions faced by corporations that involve cash or near cash are (1) cash, (2) lines of credit, and (3) the purchase of securities, where each of these decisions interacts with the others.

DECISIONS ABOUT CASH

There seem to be three basic reasons why corporations hold cash (that is, demand deposits):

1. To compensate the bank for (a) account activity, (b) financial advice

and other services provided, (c) goodwill, (d) float (collections being made by the bank), (e) lines of credit, and (f) bank loans

2. To provide for transactions involving, (a) normal operations and (b) capital expenditures

3. To provide for contingencies

The amount to be held to satisfy banks is to a great extent dependent on the amount desired by the banks. Where the bank has not clearly defined the amounts to be held for one or more of the six purposes under item 1, the amount held is a decision based on managerial judgment. The decision will depend to some extent on the bank's reaction to the balances held by the corporation in the past, and to some extent on the corporation's judgement about the amount it should hold as a demand deposit.

The procedures used by banks for pricing various services (including lines of credit and loans) sometimes obscure the actual cost. Not only is the cost of a given service hard to determine, but it is to some extent left to the conscience and judgment of the corporation treasurer. The decision about the amount of cash needed for transactions frequently requires a judgement of the amount needed to keep the bank content. This decision is further complicated by the fact that one dollar of bank balance may sometimes satisfy several balance requirements of the bank (for example the balance requirement for account activity may serve also for the line of credit requirement).

There are many stories told of firms that have either failed to predict the level of compensating balances that would satisfy their bankers or have purposely played their compensating balances as tight as possible, only to find themselves paying high interest rates for credit during consequent periods of tight money. Although most banks use a floating prime rate with points added for default risk compensation as their major rate-setting device, it would be surprising if they did not interpose some other factors such as goodwill in their interest rate-setting process. Unfortunately it is difficult to measure how much goodwill $1 of compensating balances buys with a banker.

Some corporations hold cash in anticipating of contingencies. Contingencies may be interpreted here to mean relatively minor unforeseen transactions requiring immediate cash, not major catastrophes such as depressions. The holding of cash to avoid arranging a loan for each unanticipated need for cash is reasonable. The holding of cash in anticipation of a catastrophe is not reasonable, because it would be more desirable to invest such funds in interest-earning securities. Then, too, the assumption that a corporation can or should hold liquid assets of the amount necessary to shield against the effects of a major depression is questionable.

The decisions we discuss are the determination of

1. The optimum amount of cash to be held assuming certainty about future needs
2. The optimum amount of cash to be held assuming uncertainty about future needs (i.e., imperfect knowledge of the future)
3. The amount of cash to be obtained from the market when securities are issued

The term cash is used here to refer to the total demand deposits held by one corporation, including the amount that represents compensating balances.

Assuming Certainty

Let us first assume that future needs are known with certainty, and that marketable securities can readily be converted into cash with very low transaction costs. Under these circumstances there is no need for a larger demand deposit balance than the sum of the minimum balance required by the bank plus the amount needed for the next day's transactions. If the demand deposit exceeds the value of the next day's needs, the excess may be invested. If, on the other hand, a shortage of cash holdings in relation to the next day's needs is anticipated, marketable securities may be liquidated in time to provide the funds needed.

In summary, assuming certainty, with low transaction costs it is only necessary to determine the minimum balance required by the bank plus the next day's needs. To avoid interest rate change risk, any amount in excess of this sum should be invested in securities that mature when needed; deficits in amounts needed at the time can be made up by borrowing, by allowing the demand deposit balance to go below the target balance temporarily (to be averaged against an equivalent surplus balance at some other time during the period), or by selling marketable securities. If the transaction costs are not insignificant, these costs must be balanced against the cost of holding idle funds; determining the optimal marketable securities transactions in this case is a mathematical problem we do not discuss here.[1]

Assuming Uncertainty

Since the future is rarely certain in the real world, it is necessary to investigate cash decisions assuming uncertainty. Despite the elimination of the assumption of certainty, there is no change in the decision rules just developed. As long as there is a competitive money market that the firm can enter and leave with a minimum lapse of time and with nominal cost, there is no reason to maintain cash in excess of a minimum balance. Uncertainty does affect the maximum amount of marketable securities that the corporation should hold, since it may choose to hold them as a buffer against contingencies, but the firm does not need to hold cash for these contingencies. Since the marketable securities can be liquidated almost immediately, it is only necessary to hold the sum of the minimum cash balance plus the expected needs of the next day. There remains a problem about the maturity structure of the marketable securities portfolio, but we reserve that for later discussion.

COMPUTATION OF EFFECTIVE INTEREST COST

If banks require corporations to have on deposit a compensating balance in excess of the balance that they would otherwise carry for transaction needs, the effective rate of interest becomes higher than the nominal interest rate indicated on the contract.

EXAMPLE

Assume that the bank requires that 20% of a loan be left in the bank and carried as a compensating balance. This is sometimes interpreted

[1]See H. Bierman, Jr. and J. E. Hass, *An Introduction to Managerial Finance*, New York, W. W. Norton & Co., 1973, pp. 65–70, and Yair E. Orgler, *Cash Management: Models and Methods*, Belmont, California, Wadsworth Publishing Company, Inc., 1970.

to mean that the average balance carried will be 20% of the loan and sometimes that the minimum balance will not drop below 20% of the loan. Assume now that the compensating balance results in 20% of the loan being carried as a deposit that would not otherwise be carried. Let the nominal interest rate on the loan be 8%. For a loan of $100 for a year the dollar amount of interest would be $8.

$$0.08 \times 100 = 8.00.$$

With a loan of $100, the corporation would effectively receive $80. Thus the effective rate of interest, r, is 10% since $8 of interest is being paid on an effective loan of $80.   If the corporation would normally carry the same balance with the bank, even without the requirement of a compensating balance, the real cost of the loan would be reduced to 8% with only a portion of the balance ordinarily required, the effective cost would be between 8 and 10%.

Managing the Cash Position

The demand for cash is the investment in plant, equipment, and working capital not met by internal generation of cash. The firm is likely to follow a cycle in which it first issues long-term securities (debt and equity), using some of the proceeds for immediate cash needs and investing the remainder in marketable securities. The firm then gradually sells marketable securities as their cash equivalent is demanded. The firm then turns to its banks for short- and intermediate-term credit until it is again time to issue more long-term securities.

The fundamental management problem here is the balancing of one cost against another. Although many models with much complexity have been developed to determine the optimal strategy, a brief introduction to a simple model will suffice here to demonstrate the fundamental logic. The model we use has been known for more than fifty years, but until recently was restricted in its use to physical inventory control. Assuming constant demand for the product, that the cost of ordering is independent of the size of the order, and that the cost of holding inventory increases proportionally to the average inventory, the total cost per period of providing the product (excluding the product cost itself) is

$$\text{Total cost} = \text{order costs} + \text{holding costs} \tag{1}$$

$$= K \frac{D}{Q} + k \frac{Q}{2}$$

where Q = order size each time a new order is placed (Q^* is the optimal size)

K = fixed cost incurred each time an order is placed (legal, accounting printing, etc.)

D = total demand for the product per period (say 1 year)

k = holding cost per dollar of inventory per period (same period length as used in defining total demand D). In a cash management model this is the net interest expense of long-term capital, expressed as an interest rate; it is determined by taking the cost of the long-term capital and subtracting the interest earned on marketable securities.

$Q/2$ = average inventory on hand

D/Q = number of orders per period

D/Q in the first expression of formula (1), the number of orders per period, is multiplied by the cost per order, and $Q/2$ in the second term, the average inventory carried, is multiplied by the carrying cost. The order size that minimizes the total cost is called the optimal order quantity (EOQ) and can be determined mathematically as

$$Q^* = \sqrt{\frac{2\,K\,D}{k}} \tag{2}$$

By modifying the definitions and making certain assumptions, it is possible to use this formulation to solve the cash management problem. If we assume that the firm does not employ short-term borrowing, thereby issuing long-term debt and equity whenever it has no cash or marketable securities, and further assume that marketable securities transaction costs are insignificant, thereby inferring that the firm holds no idle cash but regularly sells down its marketable securities portfolio to meet its cash needs, the EOQ formula (2) will provide the optimal amount of long-term capital to obtain in one issue.[2]

EXAMPLE

Suppose a firm that had a cash need, beyond internal generation, of $100 million per year could raise long-term capital at a 9% cost of capital and could invest idle funds in marketable securities at 7% yield. Each long-term issue had fixed costs of $90,000. Then

K = $90,000, fixed costs of issue;
D = $100,000,000, amount of cash needed per year;
k = 0.09 −0.07 = 0.02 net cost

The optimal order quantity from equation (2) is

$$Q^* = \sqrt{\frac{2 \times 90,000 \times 100,000,000}{0.02}} = \$30,000,000.$$

That is, new long-term capital should be raised in chunks of about $30 million each. The firm should issue new long-term capital slightly more frequently than three times per year. The total cost of meeting the cash needs of the firm is found from equation (1):

$$TC = \text{cost of ordering} \times \text{numbered orders}$$
$$+ \text{ net interest cost} \times \text{average near-cash balance}$$

$$TC = 90,000 \left(\frac{100,000,000}{30,000,000}\right) + 0.02 \left(\frac{30,000,000}{2}\right)$$

$$= \$300,000 + \$300,000 = \$600,000$$

Note that if the entire $100 million was obtained once per year, the total cost would be

$$TC = 90,000 \left(\frac{100,000,000}{100,000,000}\right) + 0.02 \, \frac{100,000,000}{2}$$

$$= \$1,090,000.$$

Thus the optimal strategy saves $490,000 per year!

[2]See Bierman and Hass, *op cit,* for a slightly more complicated model that allows for the possibility of transaction costs in managing the marketable securities portfolio; significant transactions costs in marketable securities result in the holding of idle cash, balancing transaction costs against interest income lost.

Following the optimal strategy, at the beginning of the period, $30,000,000 in near-cash assets will be on hand. This amount will be reduced with time as funds are used. When the amount held in marketable securities just equals the amount that will be used during the time necessary to prepare and float the new loan, the reorder process should be begun. It should be noted that the optimum order size of the amount of borrowing is affected by the square root of demand (the amount of cash needed). If the expected need for cash increased fourfold, the optimum size of a unit of borrowing would double.

Decisions About Lines of Credit

The ability to borrow bank funds at the prime rate of interest is of value to a corporation. Banks review the financial affairs of corporations frequently, however, and if the financial health of a corporation changes, the terms of its line of credit may also change. The rate of interest charged a borrower is likely to be the same whether the borrower has a line of credit or does not have one. Although a line of credit might make a loan readily available that would otherwise be difficult or impossible to obtain, it does not appear to affect significantly the terms of the loan.

During the period for which the line of credit is applicable, the corporation has ready access to bank funds. How much is this access worth? It must be remembered that having a line of credit is not a guarantee of funds during a period of prolonged hardship for the corporation. The bank will periodically review the credit relationship, and the terms of the loan (including whether a loan will be made available) will reflect the health of the corporation. The line of credit is useful in obtaining funds quickly when they are needed for operations and for contingencies likely to arise in the normal course of business, but not for a prolonged critical period in the corporation's business.

A distinction must be made between a line of credit and a credit agreement (a committed line of credit). A line of credit may not be an irrevocable commitment by the bank to make a loan. If the bank enters into a credit agreement, however, it has contracted to make a loan or loans up to the amount of the commitment and is legally obligated to do so. Even without a firm commitment, a line of credit is useful, because it may facilitate the borrowing process.

A bank extending a line of credit to a corporation, with or without a firm commitment, usually requires compensating balances. Ordinarily if the commitment is firm, there is in addition a charge based on the size of the credit agreement. This charge varies with general credit conditions, but a typical rate would be ½% of the unborrowed balance. Thus the corporation treasurer must first decide whether the corporation is willing to pay the extra charge for a firm commitment, and what the size of that commitment is. If a firm commitment is not chosen, there still remains the decision as to the size of the line of credit the corporation will attempt to obtain (the cost in this case being the opportunity cost of the amount of compensating balances the bank will request plus the cost of making the arrangement). Note that we do not discuss the direct costs of the money actually borrowed (which would probably be the same under either type of arrangement).

Costs may be associated with three separate arrangements:

1. *Costs associated with the credit agreement.* There may be costs for arranging a commitment and costs for the commitment itself. The latter may be expressed as a fixed percentage of the unborrowed portion of the amount committed and (or) as a compensating balance in some relation to the amount of the commitment.

2. *Costs associated with the line of credit.* There may be costs of negotiating the arrangement and costs of the compensating balances usually required for such an arrangement.

3. *Direct costs of borrowing.* There are usually interest costs at a specified rate on the amount borrowed plus the costs of compensating balances that may be required in some relation to the amount borrowed.

Compensating balances may be required under any of the arrangements. The direct costs of borrowing are usually the same if it is done under a credit agreement or a line of credit. If there were no costs for arrangement 1 or 2, a company would negotiate an amount equal to its highest conceivable need.

For simplicity we speak of a "line of credit," since the same basic approach applies whether we are dealing with a committed or uncommitted line of credit. Although we use the term "line of credit," we could substitute credit agreement (or committed line of credit) in those cases in which there is a firm agreement.

One can imagine a corporation having a demand curve for a line of credit. The exact shape of the demand curve for the line of credit is not of great importance for this discussion. What is important is that the indirect costs of different lines of credit be explicitly recognized. Since it is likely that the bank will require a compensating balance in addition to the regular percentage charge, the additional compensating balance should be converted into dollar cost.

From the bank's point of view, outstanding lines of credit are desirable for several reasons:

1. They provide a return to the bank, which may be in the form of compensating balances or explicit payments.
2. They tend to tie the corporation to the bank.
3. They give some indication of the loans to be expected in the coming period.

From the point of view of the corporation, the line of credit is desirable because it makes borrowing from a bank a relatively routine procedure that simplifies the job of the treasurer. Given the bank's schedule of charges, the treasurer must decide on the total amount the firm is willing to pay for this service. The actual cost that the corporation pays for services at any one time can be measured, but the benefits are more difficult to measure. Nevertheless, an attempt must be made to measure benefits also if the decision is to be consistent with the desires of the management of the corporation.

A Line of Credit Decision

We use the decision of determining the amount of a line of credit to illustrate the basic elements of decision making under uncertainty. Consider the following three components:

1. The possible decisions we may make. For example, consider the decision "how large a bank credit line is desirable." The possible decisions are the different possible credit lines ranging from zero to a very large dollar number. We assume that the presence of a line of credit ensures the obtaining of a loan if it is needed. (In actuality it may only increase the probability of obtaining the loan.)

2. The possible outcomes that may occur. One of the possible outcomes will be the actual outcome. For example, continuing the credit line example, the possible outcomes are that the need for the credit will be 0,1,2,. . . (the units may be millions or tens of millions of dollars). After the period has ended, we will be able to say that the need was X million dollars. Before the fact, we may have subjective probability estimates of the likelihood of each outcome's occurrence, that is, estimates of the probabilities of various states of nature being true.

3. For each decision and each outcome there is a consequence. For example we could have a credit line of zero units, in which case we incur zero cost if the need for credit is zero. However, if the need for credit is positive and no credit line has been arranged, the firm may incur a cost. Also, possessing a line of credit has a cost itself. If we have one unit of credit on line and the need for credit is one unit, we would incur less total cost for meeting credit needs than if the firm had a line of five units.

4. Establish a criterion (or several criteria) that will enable us to choose the best of the several eligible acts.

For decisions involving small amounts we can compute the expected cost and choose the optimum decision based on this expectation. But the expected cost omits information about specific outcomes (such as large losses) that we might want to consider before multiplying dollar amounts by a probability and summing.

In many situations it is reasonable that the decision maker accepts the criterion of computing the expected value and choosing that decision with the highest expected value. However, with large dollar amounts, the use of expected value is not necessarily consistent with intuitive preference. One of the difficulties is in the use of dollars to measure the amounts of benefits or costs that result from a set of acts and states.

Assume that there are two investments under consideration. With investment A you receive X for certain. With investment B you have a 0.5 probability of receiving $1 million and a 0.5 probability of receiving $0. What must the value of X be for you to be indifferent between the two investments? On an expected monetary value basis your answer would be $500,000, but most persons would answer differently. Now, let us ask a slightly different question. How much would you pay for the privilege of undertaking investment B? Again the answer on an expected monetary value basis would be $500,000, but most of us would not write a check for $500,000 to pay for the investment.

These examples indicate that it may not be appropriate to use the monetary expectations as the basis for decision making. There is an even more dramatic example called the St. Petersburg Paradox, which we now describe.

Assume a situation in which a fair coin is to be tossed a number of times and the amount you are to be given is equal to $\$2^n$ where n is the number of the toss on which the first head appears. The schedule of your possible winnings is as follows:

Number of tosses for First Head	Winnings	Probability of Outcome
1	$ 2	1/2
2	4	1/4
3	8	1/8
4	16	1/16
.	.	
.	.	
.	.	
n	2^n	$1/2^n$

How much would you pay to play this game? It is interesting that if we multiply the "winnings" by the probability of each event and sum the products, we find that the expected monetary value of the game is an infinite amount. However, the average person would pay considerably less that $20 to play. To make the above example even more striking, we change the winnings to 2^n pennies. The expected monetary value remains an infinite amount, but if we were willing to pay $20 previously, the amount we would invest now is considerably less.

If we cannot use the expected value of dollars in making decisions, what is an alternative? In 1944 a book, *Theory of Games and Economic Behavior* by John Von Neumann and Oskar Morgenstern, was published. The work introduced concepts that are very important to decision making; among them is the so-called concept of modern utility. By investigating a person's reactions to decisions involving risk, a relationship is obtained that enables us to convert the consequences of a decision and outcome from dollars to another measure called utility. If you were willing to pay $100,000 for the investment B described previously (0.5 probability of winning $1 million and 0.5 probability of winning $0), we would say that the utility of an outlay of $100,000 was equal (but with opposite sign) to the utility of the investment.

An important lesson to be learned is that it may be misleading to make decisions based on monetary expectations, and we are led into the use of utility in analyzing the desirability of a set of decisions. A reasonable procedure is to take the expectations of the utilities of different events and compute the expected utility of each possible decision. The decision with the greatest expected utility would be optimum. This procedure is called the "Bayes Decision Rule" and was first introduced by by Thomas Bayes in a paper titled, "An Essay Toward Solving a Problem in the Doctrine of Chance" published in 1763.

This last reference leads us to the very interesting area called statistical decision theory. Statistical decision theory relates to the problem of obtaining information about which state of nature is true, using evidence to adjust the probability distribution of the states of nature to arrive at new probabilities, and finally, taking into consideration the possible losses (or costs or profits) associated with each decision, to choose the optimum decision.

A primary importance of the techniques discussed is not necessarily in formal application in the above areas. Rather the primary benefit may be a general method of approaching a decision and a tool for explaining the reasons for reaching decision. Two perfectly reasonable persons may arrive at different decisions if they have different probability distributions associated with the possible events, or they may have different concepts of the losses associated with the events. To a great extent these two factors explain the large amount of trading done in the stock market.

One characteristic to be remembered about all decision making is that it is possible that a correct decision (consistent with the chosen criterion) will lead to an undesirable result. For example, in a line of credit problem where we want to determine the amount of the line, we can decide to arrange for a one-unit line because that act has the lowest expected cost, but then find the need for credit to be two units. This situation has an important performance measurement implication. It may be more important to judge the quality of the inputs to the decision-making process and the decision-making process itself than to look at the results of the decision. Although it is important to analyze results and learn from our mistakes, a bad outcome is not necessarily the product of a bad decision.

It is thus possible that the decision maker who had decided on one unit of credit and then incurred a cost when two units of credit were needed may have made a better decision than the financial manager who chose two units of credit and would have incurred less costs in the same situation.

A possible and unfortunate result of this reasonable approach to performance evaluation is that it weakens the ability of top management to jump to conclusions about the performance of their subordinates, but this difficulty is a fact of life in the world of uncertainty, the world in which we all must operate.

DECISIONS ABOUT SECURITIES

The acquisition of cash resources by issuing long-term capital generally leads to a temporary excess of cash available for investment in marketable securities. Four kinds of decisions must be made before investing in securities, namely:

1. How much cash to invest in securities
2. The timing of security purchases
3. The composition of the securities portfolio
4. The maturity dates of the securities

The amount held in securities is a residual decision, that is, the result of other decisions such as the amount of cash to be held, dividend policy, and internal investment policy (investment in real assets).

There are several reasons for a corporation to hold marketable securities:

1. In anticipation of monthly or seasonal transaction needs. For example, a firm may make collections on the tenth of the month but not have payments until the end of the month. The funds may be invested for 20 days. Another example would be in anticipation of an income tax payment. Payment of taxes rarely coincides with cash flow into the firm. The company might prefer to leave the cash in the bank. The decision depends on several factors, includ-

ing the costs of making investments, the current interest rates, the present deposit balance, the income credit rate, and the state of the corporation's relations with the bank.

2. In anticipation of internal investments.

3. In order to maintain current dividend policy.

4. In anticipation of possible adverse business conditions (contingencies).

The last two reasons are based on assumptions about stockholder preferences. Some stockholders would prefer the corporation to hold securities in order to accomplish a stabilization of dividends or to avoid embarrassment if business conditions are not good. Others would prefer that the corporation either invest the funds internally or, if suitable internal investments were not available, distribute the funds to them.

If we agree that securities may rightly be purchased in anticipation of future transaction needs, the problem reverts back to determining the optimum amount of cash to be held, any excess being invested in securities and a shortage being made up through short-term borrowing. From the bank's point of view there is some disadvantage in a corporation's borrowing without warning, especially where the bank has to adjust its reserve position to take care of the loan request. Sudden borrowing may have an implicit cost for the bank.

Given a decision to hold X dollars of marketable securities, there remains a problem about the maturity structure of the marketable securities portfolio. The longer the maturity, the more severe the response of the market price of the securities to a change in market interest rates. If the firm must sell a security prior to its maturity date to meet its cash needs, but interest rates have risen since the security was purchased, the security will sell for less than the price at which it was purchased. Although the reverse also holds true, thus allowing the possibility of a capital gain rather than loss as a result of interest rate changes, treasurers are reluctant to hold securities with maturities that exceed the time it is expected the cash will be needed. When it is not clear how long it will be until it will be needed, the usual policy is to hold short-term securities that are then "rolled-over" when they mature, or arrange a "cascade" portfolio structure with securities maturing at regular intervals. Since a security at (or near) maturity sells for (approximately) face value, the interest rate risk tends to be avoided by this strategy.

In addition to different maturities, there are also different types of securities in which a corporation may invest, many (such as commerical paper) which offer higher returns than securities of the federal government (consistent with their greater risk). The composition of the portfolio of a particular corporation would depend on other characteristics of the corporation (such as its capital structure) and the risk preferences of the individual officers. In many corporations the board of directors specifies the types of securities that are eligible for investment, and in most corporations a senior officer must approve the investment.

It is reasonable for a corporation to invest in long-term securities or in securities other than those of the federal government and bear the accompanying risk if the management thinks that their higher interest as compared to interest on short-term federal government securities makes the expected return outweigh the risk. It is desirable that management have enough flexibility to take advantage of such opportunities, but management should also be aware that investing in these types of securities results in an additional source of risk for the corporation.

Although some managements follow a hedge policy of buying securities that mature on a date close to that which the funds are expected to be needed, this policy may not always be profit maximizing; there may be occasions when a security that matures after the date that the funds are needed would be more desirable. This security could be sold on the exact date the funds are needed, but the firm would be speculating relative to future interest rate changes.

In view of the low costs of making investments, it would seem desirable to invest funds, if only for one day. One deterrent to investments in securities seems to be the desire to hold cash in the bank to gain the bank's goodwill. This argument is difficult to counter because we do not know the dollar value of the goodwill nor do we know how much it will change with a change in the amount of demand deposits.

CREDIT DECISIONS

Credit decisions are interesting because they give us an opportunity to consider the interrelationships of finance and other areas of operations, such as marketing and production. There is evidence that the top management of corporations neglects credit decisions with the result that in many situations the decisions are made by the wrong persons, with the wrong objectives in mind, based on the wrong set of information. Credit decisions are frequently made by a relatively low level of management and only reviewed when some major event occurs, for example, when it becomes obvious that uncollectable accounts have reached disastrous proportions, or when the marketing manager complains about the number of customers who have been refused credit.

We consider a basic credit decision involving a one-shot sale and known costs where either the entire amount will be paid or nothing. Complications can be readily introduced, but they would merely distract from major components of the decision. Let the probability of collection be p and the amount to be collected $100. If the incremental cost of making the sale is $60, then the sale is desirable if 100 p is greater than $60, or p is greater than 0.6. Thus the critical probability is 0.6. If the incremental cost of making the sale were larger or smaller than $60, the critical probability would also change.

Banks work with a very small margin and cannot afford to risk not being paid when they make loans. The critical probability for a bank is very large.

A manufacturing firm has an interesting set of credit decisions because, if the firm has slack in its production capacity, credit can be offered to relatively weak customers, since the relevant cost should include only the incremental costs. However, if demand for its products increases so that the firm is operating at capacity, the cost of accepting a bad credit risk is the expected total revenues lost from a good customer (this is the opportunity cost).

It is important that manufacturing, sales, and credit departments are in direct communication with each other so that the credit department can make decisions consistent with the current demand and cost situation of the firm.

We have only considered the one-shot credit decision. It is possible to expand the problem to include the future consequences of the present decision. This expanded problem lends itself to a dynamic programming solution.[3]

[3]See H. Bierman, Jr. and W. H. Hausman, "The Credit Granting Decision," *Management Science*, April 1970, B-519–B-532.

INVENTORY DECISIONS

A large portion of the literature of management science has been devoted to inventory decisions. The models start with the certainty model given earlier in this chapter (the economic order quantity or EOQ model):

$$Q = \sqrt{\frac{2\,K\,D}{k}}$$

and proceed to consider production strategies when the replacement of inventory is not instantaneous. Finally it is necessary to allow demand and other factors to be uncertain. With uncertainty comes the necessity of determining the amount of inventory that should be kept as a buffer stock. The buffer stock protects the firm against shortages arising because demand during the reorder period is higher than expected or because the reorder period is longer than expected.

It is not the purpose of this book to describe in detail the many different models that can be used to help make inventory decisions. It is only necessary for the reader to know that they exist. If inventory decisions are being made, the decision maker should be familiar with them.[4]

Assuming that sophisticated models are being used to make inventory decisions, it is important that the performance of the decision maker not be evaluated using naive measures of inventory turnover. For example, a high turnover may be undesirable from a decision standpoint (a low inventory may result in a high turnover, but sales are lost because inventory is not available). In like manner, a record of no shortages, rather than indicating an alert inventory policy, may actually reflect a situation in which excessive inventory is being carried by the firm. Here again, costs must be weighed; in this case it is the cost of a lost sale versus the cost of holding higher inventories.

[4]Two good books on inventory models are M. K. Starr and D. W. Miller, *Inventory Control: Theory and Practice,* Englewood Cliffs, N. J.: Prentice-Hall., Inc., 1962, and by the same publisher, H. M. Wagner, *Principles of Operations Research,* 1969.

ACCOUNTS PAYABLE AND SHORT-TERM BORROWING

The theory of administration of accounts payable is simple. Payments should be made as late as feasible consistent with the terms of the purchase contract. The funds not paid out can, of course, be invested. When there is a penalty associated with late payment, the penalty is usually of a punitive nature and should in general be avoided. The penalty may be in the form of a lost discount, or it may be an interest charge. The form of the penalty does not make a difference, but the amount does. For example, assume the terms of sale are such that there is a 1% discount if the account is paid within 20 days, but the total (gross) amount must be paid after 30 days, with additional penalties occurring after 30 days. Thus the firm that does not pay on day 20 pays 1% for the use of funds for 10 days. This is equivalent to an annual rate of approximately 36%. Most firms can borrow short-term funds at a rate cheaper than 36% and should not lose the discount.

Shifting our attention from trade accounts to short-term borrowing, there are two basic strategies that can be followed by a firm. First, the firm can borrow short term until the short-term borrowing capacity is exhausted, and then the firm can shift to a long-term financing. Second, the firm can follow a policy where by the firm borrows long term in anticipation of the cash needs; it then has funds available for short-term investment.

The optimum strategy for a firm is likely to be part way between the two situations described. That is, a firm is likely to find it desirable to use short-term financing and then float a large long-term loan that results in excess cash. When that cash is used, the firm can again use short-term financing until it is more desirable to again use long-term debt.

Where the cash needs of a firm are seasonal, the firm has another related decision. This decision is illustrated in Fig. 2.1. Strategy 1 has sufficient permanent capital so that the seasonal needs are met by internal resources. When there is slack, the excess cash is invested in short-term securities. Strategy 2 has a minimum of long-term capital, and seasonal needs are satisfied by short-term borrowing.

Thus short-term borrowing has three basic uses. It may serve as a substitute for a buffer stock of working capital against financial crises; it may be used in sequence with long-term debt to supply the cash needed to finance the growth of a firm; it can be used to supply the temporary (seasonal) cash needs of a firm.

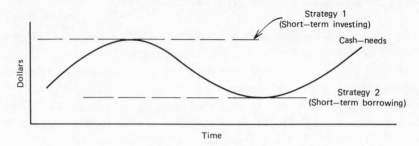

Figure 2.1.   Two financial strategies.

In addition to bank loans, large corporations may issue their own private IOU's called commercial paper. Commercial paper is short-term (less than a a year) borrowing backed by the overall credit of the firm. The explicit cost of the commercial paper is likely to be somewhat less than the cost of a bank loan that includes a compensating balance; thus there is an economic incentive for well-established firms to use this financing device. The disadvantage of commercial paper is that, unlike a bank loan, once it is outstanding it remains outstanding until maturity (a bank loan may be repaid at an earlier date than the maturity date). Thus if its cash needs change, a firm can be locked into a debt with commercial paper; this is not as bad as it sounds because the funds can be invested in some other firm's paper, more or less balancing the interest revenue and expense.

A prime advantage of commercial paper is that a well-established firm can raise millions of dollars quickly. It may only take a phone call to a commercial paper dealer to arrange the financing (the dealer then makes calls to place the paper with firms possessing temporary excess cash). Of course, the use of commercial paper is limited to firms with exceptionally good credit standings. This limitation does not preclude periodic defaults by firms that have issued paper; thus it should not be thought that commercial paper does not have its risks from the point of view of investors.

FINANCIAL PLANNING

There is an interesting conflict of incentives involving working capital. If cash, accounts receivable, and inventory are administrated independent of each other in an efficient manner, this could result in the firm having a relatively small amount of working capital. A small amount of working capital could result in the firm being excessively vulnerable to small cash flow difficulties that might arise. For example, assume that earnings before interest and taxes (X) has the probability distribution as shown in Fig. 2.2. The area under the curve represents probability.

With a low level of working capital, we can assume that earnings before interest and taxes of b (where b is some negative income) will result in major financial difficulties. However, with a larger amount of working capital it is possible that income must fall to a level of d before the firm is in difficulty. Inspection fo Figure 2.2 shows that the probability of income being less than b is approximately twice the probability of income being less than d. Working capital can act as a buffer against unexpected financial difficulties. However, keeping working capital in excess of that dictated by the optimization models has a capital cost. One alternative is for the firm to have credit agreement with a bank (that is, a firm agreement enabling it to borrow). This alternative might have a lower cost than maintaining the excess working capital.

Since working capital tends to be relatively liquid, a firm that makes errors in working capital decisions by accumulating excessive amounts can usually rectify them easily compared to the errors it makes when it invests funds in unprofitable long-lived assets. Nevertheless, working capital decisions should not be neglected. Changes in credit or inventory policy may drastically affect sales and profits, and yet these effects

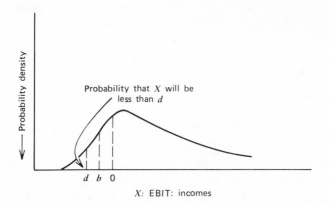

Figure 2.2. Income is uncertain.

may not be obvious. The decisions involving working capital are somewhat like an iceberg. The consequences that are below the surface (e.g., the sales lost) may not be apparent to the eye.

The consequences of working capital policies and decisions should be fully understood by management. In like manner, the effect of long-lived asset decisions on working capital should also be understood. If a new plant for new products is to be built, part of the investment in the new plant is the additional cash that will have to be on deposit in the bank, the inventory that will have to be carried, and accounts receivable that will have to be financed. To be effective, financial planning must consider not only the dollars committed to the purchase of plant and equipment, but also the dollars committed to supplying the working capital necessary to operate the long-lived assets.

CONCLUSIONS

We have surveyed several aspects of working capital decisions, but the reader should not assume that we have completely covered the subject. For example, in Chapter 3 we consider decision making where time is an important factor.

The St. Petersburg paradox highlights the necessity of a firm considering other factors than the average outcome (the expectation). Risk analysis is a necessary component of all decision making where there is a significant amount of uncertainty. In this chapter the need to consider the "utility of outcomes" was introduced. Future chapters suggest that under some conditions market factors may be used to bypass the difficult task of applying utility theory in the real world.

In the future we can expect decision making to become more quantitative in the sense that more models will be built to aid in decision processes, and more data will be presented to administrators. However, one should not expect to find a world in which judgment and emotion are completely removed from the decision process. At best, the quantitative models of the future will incorporate systematically the judgments of the decision makers so that they may be brought to bear on the decision. Rather than being eliminated, the administrators' insights and experience will be extended in a manner that will more effectively bring their desires and knowledge into the decision process.

CHAPTER 3

CAPITAL BUDGETING

Ignore emotion, impulse, and less important facts.
Smart managers are using present value after tax.

Capital budgeting is a term used to describe the analysis of incremental cash flows arising from managerial decision making. Capital budgeting decisions generally involve outlays that are immediate (or nearly immediate) and benefits that are stretched out through time. In some cases the benefits may be deferred for many years. The primary problem facing management in capital budgeting is to incorporate timing and risk considerations in such a manner that the well-being of the stockholder is maximized.

The importance of good capital budgeting procedures is highlighted in situations in which they are lacking. For example, New York State agencies have borrowed funds using long-term debt to finance investments that will not generate the cash needed to repay the debt and, because of their nature, could not be expected to repay the debt. In another situation, a company built a plant that could not be profitable even if it operated 24 hours a day. Reasonable capital budgeting procedures should have indicated the undesirable nature of these projects.

CLASSIFICATION OF CAPITAL BUDGETING DECISIONS

We find it useful to classify investment decisions into three types:

1. Making accept or reject decisions involving investments whose cash flows are independent of each other.

2. Choosing the best of a set of mutually exclusive investments; that is, because of their characteristics only one of the investments can be undertaken (for example, you only place one roof on a plant).
3. Ranking of investments in order of their desirability.

This third classification requires explanation. Although investments can be ranked subjectively in the same manner that one can rank the ten best movies of the year, there is no perfectly reliable objective way to rank investments. This disclosure is generally disappointing to managers who like to rank investments in order of relative desirability and then cut off when all investable funds are committed. In fact, some "solutions" have been offered that claim to accomplish such rankings. Unfortunately, no general solution exists other than systematic enumeration. In some very well-defined situations, correct ranking can be achieved using an index method, but these situations are not likely to be frequently encountered in the real world, thus again the rankings are approximate.

However, all is not lost. Most important, we know how to separate investments into two classifications, acceptable and not acceptable. If a manager then wants to rank the acceptable investments using subjective or quasiquantitative techniques, given the degree of uncertainty that exists in the world, this practice is apt to be useful, if the limitations are noted. Secondly, the need for a ranking can be avoided by a "programming" technique that choses the best set of investments, given the resource limitations, that maximizes the measure (say, present value) that management wants to maximize.

TIME VALUE

It is well known that money has value and that a dollar in hand today is worth more than a dollar to be received one year from today. For example, if money can be borrowed and lent at 10% per year, then $100 held today and invested to earn 10% will be worth $110 one year from today. In like manner, $100 to be received one year from today has a present value of $90.91 ($90.91 invested to earn 10% will earn $9.09 interest and will be worth $100 after one year).

Assuming that we can borrow and lend at an interest rate of r, the following variant of the compound interest formula enables us to move future cash flows back through time to the present:

$$A = S (1 + r)^{-n},$$

where r = the interest rate
n = the number of time periods
S = the future sum to be received at the end of the nth period from now
A = the present value or present equivalent of the future S.

If r, n, and S are properly specified, then one is indifferent between S dollars at time n and A dollars now. The factor $(1 + r)^{-n}$ is called the present value factor. It transforms future sums into present value equivalents (see Table A in the appendix).

For example, assume a firm is offered a security that will pay $1 million two years from now, and the firm can earn 10 percent on other investments. Since the present value factor is $(1.10)^{-2} = 0.826446$, the present value of the $1 million is

$$A = 1,000,000 (1.1)^{-2} = 1,000,000 (.826446) = \$826,446.$$

The firm is indifferent between $826,446 now and the security offering $1 million two years from now. The following calculations demonstrate the firm's indifference if the present value can be invested to earn the stated interest rate:

Initial sum	$826,446
1st year interest (10%)	82,645
Balance, end year one	909,091
2nd year interest (10%)	90,909
Sum after two years	$1,000,000

The present value factor, $(1 + r)^{-n}$, takes on different values for various r and n. These values have been tabulated and appear in Table A at the end of this book. To find the present equivalent at interest rate r of a future sum S received at the end of period n, one simply multiplies S by the corresponding present value factor from Table A.

Quite often one is required to find the present value of a stream of cash flows. This can always be accomplished by summing the present equivalent of each item in the stream. However, when the items are identical in nominal value (this is termed an "annuity"), a special formula or tables make the computation much easier. If a dollar is to be received at the end of each period for n periods and the appropriate discount rate is r, the present value of the stream of dollars is

$$B(n,r) = \left[1 - (1 + r)^{-n} \right]/r.$$

Table B at the end of the book lists the values of $B(n,r)$ for various combinations of n and r. In the special case in which a one dollar per period of annuity goes on forever (n equals infinity), the present value of that annuity is $1/r$. For example, the present value of $100 per year for 20 years at 10% is

$$\text{present value} = 100 \times B(20,0.10) = 100 \times 8.5136 = \$851.36$$

A perpetuity of $100 would have a present value of

$$\text{present value} = 100/0.10 = \$1000$$

at the same 10% discount rate.

Note that $B(n,r)$ can also be determined by summing the first n entries under discount rate r of Table A. Thus $B(2,0.10) = 0.9091 + 0.8264 = 1.7355$. A dollar a period for two periods, discounted at 10%, with the first dollar being received one period from now, is worth $1.7355.

METHODS OF CAPITAL BUDGETING

There are many methods of capital budgeting used by business firms, but most of them are based on one of four methods to be described here.

One must be careful of terminology in this area. The same words are used differently by different people (including authors). In this book terms are used consistently, but this does not mean that the next time you encounter the terms they will be used in the same manner as they are used here.

Probably the most widely used statistic in making investment decisions is the "payback period." The length of time required to recover the initial investment is computed, and this measure is deemed acceptable or unacceptable when compared to some maximum payback period. For example, an investment costing $1 million and recovering $250,000 per year in after-tax cash flow would have a payback period of 4 years.

The payback period criterion has two major shortcomings: (1) it fails to consider the time value of money during the payback period of the investment, and (2) it ignores all the cash flows of the investment beyond the payback period. These limitations are usually realized by well-informed managers, but many managers still use the criterion and justify its usage on risk-avoidance grounds, arguing that the shorter the payback period, the smaller the exposure to risk. Unfortunately, this is not always true. An oil refinery investment might have a relatively long payback period but be much less risky than an investment in exploration of a yet-to-be-discovered field, even though the expected payback period of the latter is only a short time.

Another popular method of measuring the profitability of an investment (although it is rapidly losing ground to better measures) is return on investment (ROI). The ROI of an investment is the average income divided by the average investment. Since the income and investment measures used are conventional accounting measures, the ROI measure fails to take effectively into consideration the time value of money. The conventional ROI measure is a very unreliable way of evaluating investments. However, there is an even worse way of applying the technique. A common practice in industry is to compute the ROI of the first complete year of use. Since this ROI, as conventionally computed, will tend to *understate* the true rate of return on investment, this creates a bias against accepting investments that should be accepted. Finally, even if some average ROI over the project life is employed, the resultant statistic can still be misleading, because most managements interpret it as the DCF rate of return on the investment, which it will be only by accident (DCF refers to discounted cash flow).

To illustrate these problems, consider a $9,000 investment proposal that would result in the following set of cash flows:

		Year		
	0	1	2	3
Sales		$8000	$8000	$8000
Out-of-pocket costs		3000	3000	3000
Gross margin		5000	5000	5000
Depreciation (sum-of-years digits method)		4500	3000	1500
Earning before tax		500	2000	3500
Tax (40% tax rate)		200	800	1400
Net income		$300	$1200	$2100
Cash flow[1]	−$9000	$4800	$4200	$3600
Average investment		$7500	$4500	$1500
ROI (net income average investment)		4%	26%	140%

[1]Cash flow is the net income plus depreciation in this example.

The discounted rate of return on this investment is 20% per annum; that is, 20% is the compound interest yield on the funds invested in the project. Yet the first year ROI is far too low, and the average ROI of the three years is far too high (approximately 57%). ROI may be simple, but it is elusive and misleading; unless it is carefully computed.

The other methods that require explanation are the several discounted cash flow measures. These measures are more reliable measures of value than the payback and ROI measures previously described. The discussion in this chapter is limited to the rate of return and the present value methods. These two measures are chosen because they are widely used and also because in making accept or reject decisions, they will do everything that alternative methods will do and in some cases will avoid errors introduced by the other measures.

THE PRESENT VALUE METHOD

The present value method of evaluating investments has been increasing in use for the past 20 years. It is now difficult to find a Fortune 500 firm that does not employ the present value method (generally used in conjunction with other measures) somewhere in its organization.

The first step in the computation of the net present value of an investment is to choose a rate of discount, often called the "hurdle rate." The second step is to compute the present value equivalents of all cash flows associated with the investment (on an after-tax basis) and sum these present value equivalents to obtain the net present of the investment.

The net present value of an investment is the amount the firm could afford to pay in excess of the cost of the investment and still break even on the investment. It is also the present value of all future profits, where the profits are after the recovery of the capital costs of the investment. We can say that it measures the net economic benefit to stockholders of undertaking the investment. It is an excellent summary measure of investment value.

EXAMPLE

Consider an investment costing $902,740 that promises cash flows of $1 million one period from now and $100,000 two periods from now. Using the present value factors for $r = 0.10$ from Table A we have

Time Period	Cash Flows	Present Value Factors (0.10)	Present Value Equivalents
0	−902,740	1.0000	−902,740
1	1,000,000	0.9091	909,100
2	100,000	0.8264	82,640
		Net Present Value	$ 89,000

The firm could pay $89,000 more than the $902,740 cost and break-even (that is, would then just earn the 0.10 capital cost). Thus the $89,000 is, in a sense, the "excess" incentive to invest and is a measure of the safety margin. These statements do assume a zero tax rate.

Let us assume the following arbitrary depreciation schedule (any other schedule would give the same present value of income if the interest on book value is deducted):

Year	Depreciation
1	842,740
2	60,000

The following incomes then result:

Year	Revenues	Depreciation	Income before Interest	Interest on Book Value	Income after Interest	Present Value Factors	Present Value
1	1,000,000	842,740	157,260	90,274	66,986	.9091	60,900
2	100,000	60,000	40,000	6,000	34,000	.8264	28,100

Present Value of Incomes $89,000

The present value of the after interest incomes is $89,000, which is the amount of net present value obtained above.

The argument is sometimes offered that the present value method is difficult to understand. Actually it is the simplest procedure to use. If the net present value is positive, the investment is acceptable. Also, the interpretation of the measure is easy and useful. The net present value is the amount the firm could pay in excess of the cost and still break even, and it is the present value of the incomes after capital costs are recovered. It is a measure of the benefit to the firm (stockholders) of undertaking an investment, with the benefit expressed in terms of present value.

THE RATE OF RETURN METHOD

The present value method gives a dollar measure. Some managers prefer a percentage measure that is most frequently called an investment's rate of return. Other terms applied to the same measure are yield, DCF or discounted cash flow, return on investment, time adjusted rate of return, profitability index, and to complete the circle, present value.

We can define the rate of return as the rate of discount that causes the sum of the present values of the cash flows to be equal to zero. This definition can then be used to compute an investment's rate of return. The rate of return is found by a trial and error procedure (when the net present value is equal to zero, the rate of discount being used is the rate of return).

Continuing the above example, we find that the net present value is equal to zero using a 0.20 rate of discount. For discount rates larger than 0.20, the net present value would be negative.

Present Values with Different Discount Rates

Time	Present Value 0%	Present Value 10%		Present Value 20%	
0	−902,740	1.0000	−902,740	1.0000	−902,740
1	1,000,000	.9091	909,100	0.8333	833,300
2	100,000	.8264	82,640	0.6944	69,440
Net Present Value	+197,260		+89,000		0

The rate of return of an investment has several interesting and relevant economic interpretations. For example, it is the highest rate that the firm can borrow, use the funds generated by the investment, and repay the loan. Assume funds are borrowed at a cost of .20. The following repayment schedule would then apply:

Initial amount owed	$ 902,800
Year one interest (0.20)	+180,500
Principal plus interest, end of year	1,083,300
Repayment using cash flows	−1,000,000
Balance due, end of year	83,300
Year two interest (0.20)	+ 16,700
Principal plus interest, end of year	$ 100,000
Repayment using cash flows	$ 100,000
Amount owed	0

The cash flows generated by the investment are just sufficient to pay the loan costing 0.20.

If incomes and investments are properly measured, the ROI (that is, income divided by investment) of each year will be equal to the rate of return of the investment, but this will not occur using conventional accounting. Chapter 5 offers a more complete explanation and justification for this claim.

The decision rule to be used with the rate of return method is that all investments with a rate of return greater than the required return (hurdle rate) be accepted (this assumes the cash flows are those of a normal investment, that is, one or more periods of cash outlays followed by cash inflows.)

THE NET PRESENT VALUE PROFILE

For any investment we can compute its net present value profile. Figure 3.1 shows the net present value profile for the example of this chapter. The different rates of discount are measured on the X axis, the net present value that results from the use of the different rates of discount on the Y axis. The intersection of the net present value profile and the X axis defines the rate of return of the investment (the point at which the net present value is equal to zero).

Inspection of Figure 3.1 shows that for a normal investment the present value profile slopes downward to the right. Thus for an investment with a rate of return greater than the required return, the net present value will also be positive. Hence with normal independent investments having outlays followed by positive cash flows the present value method (a dollar measure) and the rate of return method (a percentage) will give identical accept/reject decisions.

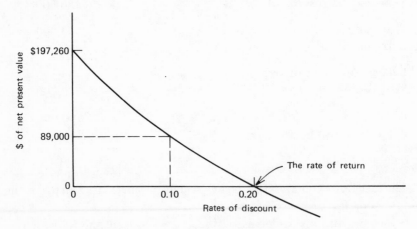

Figure 3.1. Profile of net present value for investment.

MUTUALLY EXCLUSIVE INVESTMENTS

In the situation in which one is to choose the best of a set of mutually exclusive investments, the operating characteristics of the investments are such that only one can be taken. For example, the alternatives may be different sized electric generating plants, and only one is to be constructed. In such a decision-making situation, it is important to realize the relationship between the rate of return and present value methods of investment analysis.

The most important distinction between the two is that the rate of return analysis does not carry any indication of the size of the investment; it is a percentage. Thus one may actually prefer a lower rate of return if the lower rate of return alternative has many more dollars invested. For example, suppose the firm can invest funds elsewhere at 10% (which then becomes the relevant hurdle rate) and is trying to decide between investments A and B, which are expected to produce the following results:

| | Cash Flows | | Rate of | Present Value |
	Period 0	Period 1	Return	10%
Investment A	-10,000	14,000	0.40	1273
Investment B	-55,000	66,000	0.20	5001

Figure 3.2 summarizes this information.

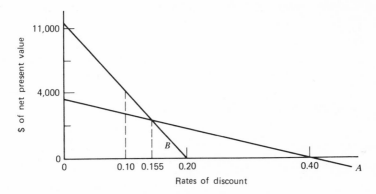

Figure 3.2.   Two mutually exclusive investments.

At a hurdle rate of 10%, there is a clear preference for investment B, even though it has the lower rate of return. Why? Because investment B has $55,000 earning 20%, whereas A has only $10,000 earning 40% (and the remaining $45,000 earning only 10%, the hurdle rate). Thus the rate of return criterion can be misleading in the case of mutually exclusive investment decision making.

An alternative approach to the same conclusion is to examine the incremental investment from A to B. That is, having determined that A is preferable to doing nothing, is it profitable to increment up to B? This would require an additional $45,000 outlay and would generate an additional $52,000 inflow a year later; that works out to be a 15.5% rate of return on the incremental investment, which is well above the 10% hurdle rate and again shows B preferable to A.

USE OF CASH FLOWS

Most analysts now agree that the appropriate measure of an investment's value should be derived from the incremental cash flows that would occur if the investment were undertaken. Although there is some reliance on accounting conventions in the determination of the tax consequences of the investment, incremental cash flow analysis is not fundamentally dependent on accounting accruals and assumptions. Cash flows are a clearly measurable and unquestionably important measure of a firm's economic well-being.

Although debt financing may be used in the firm's capital structure, debt cash flows are generally excluded from a cash flow analysis, thus making the measures obtained independent of the method of financing. For some purposes the decision maker may wish to include all the debt cash flows (not just interest payments) to obtain profitability measures on stockholder equity. Care must be taken in the comparative use of any such measure, since the measure is clearly dependent on the amount of debt financing factored into the analysis.

CAPITAL BUDGETING AND PLANNING

The capital budgets through time of a firm are a primary input into any planning document, since the investment decisions determine the cash needs of the firm and thus the amount of capital that must be raised. The investments that are undertaken will in turn influence both the amount and the reliability of the cash flow stream in the future.

Although a capital budget should be an integral part of a long-range plan, there are few investment decisions that cannot be modified if the external environment changes. For example, an automobile company may plan in 1973 to build a plant to produce large automobiles begin- and a resulting change in consumer preferences and government legislation.

However, when a corporation has actually expended the funds for an investment project with a long life, it is frequently difficult for the firm to do anything except operate the asset. Thus the investment decisions of yesterday and today greatly affect the financial plans for the future.

Although the costs already incurred are "sunk" and thus properly do not affect decisions, it is frequently difficult for management to face up to past errors, dispose of mistakes, and recognize the accounting losses immediately. Second, once an asset has been acquired and the acquisition costs are "sunk," it may be in the stockholders' best interests to operate it (the incremental-revenues exceed the incremental costs) even if the accounting reports, reflecting full costs, will indicate losses.

THE CASE OF THE CONFLICTING OBJECTIVES

The following is a true case with the facts disguised. The ABC Company's research and development group had developed a new product that seemed to have great commerical appeal. The planning group of the company came up with a ten-year plan for investment to develop the product. The plan involved the construction of a pilot plant costing $6 million. If the process and product were successful, larger plants would be built, starting in year three, over the next seven years, with a total expenditure of $40 million. This plan had a positive present value and a suitable discounted rate of return. However, no sooner was the original investment recovered than an additional investment was undertaken. This resulted in a payback period of seven years, which was in excess of the allowed payback period. In addition, it was five years before the effect on earnings per share was positive.

At the request of the corporate president, a second plan was developed that incurred the entire $40,000,000 construction immediately. This plan qualified using present value, rate of return, payback, and return on average investment. However, the corporate financial vice-president objected to spending $40 million on a plant to produce a product that had never been produced commercially, and for which there was some uncertainty about the market, because the product had never been sold. The first plan was preferred.

It was obvious to the company's board of directors that the first plan was not acceptable because of the payback duration and the effect of the investment on earnings per share in the immediate years. The second plan was not acceptable because it was too risky.

The company decided to sell the patents for the new product to another firm; this firm had different investment criteria, and implemented the first plan.

It has been several years since this actual case was first encountered, and it has been told to many management seminars. In 50% of the seminars in which it has been told, someone has come up after the presentation and said that they knew the name of the firm. In each case they have been wrong.

THIS CHAPTER'S SCOPE

Capital budgeting is too big a subject to be covered in one chapter. The objective of this chapter is to make clear the nature and uses of the basic discounted cash flow methods. Complexities in their use have been omitted, as have descriptions of alternative, but inferior, calculations.[2] Too frequently managers have been unnecessarily confused about the basic nature of the present value and rate of return methods, and have consequently shown a reluctance to use them.

In the real world, top management, in addition to the measures suggested in this chapter, might want to know how an investment would affect earnings per share and the division or firm's return on investment. It can properly be argued that if the DCF methods of this chapter indicate an investment should be undertaken, the fact that

---

[2]See H. Bierman, Jr. and S. Smidt, *The Capital Budgeting Decision*, 4th ed. Macmillan, 1975, for an expansion of this material.

earnings per share and ROI computations are adversely affected in the short run should not affect the decision. However, this requires an enlightened management and well-informed shareholders.

Finally, the most important omission of this chapter is that risk is not explicitly discussed. This is rectified in Chapter 14.

CHAPTER 4

THE USE OF ROI FOR PERFORMANCE MEASUREMENT

To discover how effectively you employ
A particular asset that you currently enjoy
Use ROI, for it will measure
Your degree of gloom or your amount of pleasure.

There are several controversies raging in the literature on performance measurement and control, and it is easy to confuse the ROI (return on investment) issue with difficulties that are only tangentally related to ROI.[1] It is desirable first to consider the use of ROI without including other questionable practices. For example, one managerial problem requiring a solution is the measurement of the performance of a completely self-contained operating unit (the unit manufactures and sells its own product). Is ROI useful in this context? It can be. A critic of ROI would prefer that we consider a multidivisional firm with interconnecting transactions among the divisions that give rise to the necessity for transfer pricing and the presence of assets that are used jointly by several divisions.[2] Admittedly there are problems with a multidivisional firm in addition to the question of whether ROI is

---

[1] The following is a sample of the current literature. John Dearden, "The Case Against ROI Control," *Harvard Business Review* May-June, 1969. Six other articles by Dearden on this subject are listed in the same HBR issue. David Solomons, *Division Performance: Measurement and Control* (Financial Executives Research Foundation, 1965). Keith Schwayder,"A Proposed Modification to Residual Income—Interest Adjusted Income," *The Accounting Review*, April 1970, pp. 299–307.

[2] The reader is referred to the two classic articles on transfer pricing by Jack Hirshleifer, "On the Economics of Transfer Pricing," *Journal of Business*, July 1956, pp. 172-184 and "Economics of the Divisionalized Firm," *Journal of Business*, April 1957, pp. 96–108.

useful. For example, there is the question about whether the organization of a firm should be on a decentralized or centralized basis. Any multidivisional firm can be turned into a completely self-contained unit by doing away with profit centers, and by considering the entire corporation as an operating entity. The arguments of this chapter are limited to discussing either entire firms, self-contained operating components of a firm, or components that are not self-contained but in which there is a reasonable transfer pricing procedure.

Although the desirability of profit centers, indeed the entire question of centralization versus decentralization, is to a large extent separate from whether or not to utilize ROI, in one sense the issues merge. To compute the ROI of an operating unit, it is necessary to arrive at an income measure. This implies that the unit's product is sold, and the revenue and expense can be measured in a useful manner.

Advocating the use of ROI implies that it is a better measure of performance than is obtained from using just the income of the product being manufactured. However, one can argue in favor of the use of ROI in a specific situation without taking the position that all subsidiary operating units should be judged using ROI. For many operating units, marketing efforts are not autonomous, and it is more appropriate to use cost minimization rather than profit maximization (or its near equivalent, maximization of ROI, subject to constraints).

Although it may be true that some managers tend to place excessive faith in a ROI measure, and that the measurement of performance (so that the measure actually reflects performance) is much more difficult than is sometimes assumed. But we cannot conclude that a ROI measure is not useful. It should be realized that ROI is not necessarily the best or only measure of performance, but that ROI can be a very useful measure. Consider what a good ROI measure can accomplish. We have first a measure of income; but before concluding that the income level is satisfactory, we relate the income of the amount of assets used to earn the income. The necessity of making this comparison is obvious ($1 million of earnings may be termed to be very good, but if you are told that the operating unit used $100 million of capital to earn the $1 million, your conclusion might well shift from good to bad). To evaluate performance it is necessary to consider the amount of assets used in earning the income.

The use of ROI to evaluate performance can affect investment decisions because the manager knows that after accepting an investment its operations will affect the measurement of his performance. This leads to an incentive for the divisional (or other subcomponent) manager to reject investments that yield a lower return on investment than is being earned on the currently owned assets. Not only should top management be concerned with the return on investment of the assets being used, but also the growth in assets and income. *Growth* as well as return on investment is important. A static division earning a 30% ROI may well be evaluated as being badly managed, whereas it may be concluded that a division that is growing and earning 15% is well managed.

The investment decision problem resulting from a desire to maintain a high ROI highlights the necessity of not relying on one performance measure (ROI or something else) but rather bringing in sufficient measures to restrain the impulse of persons trying to circumvent the control-evaluation system.

We can dispose of a wide range of possible criticisms of ROI as a means of evaluating investment proposals by arguing that there are better methods of making investments.[3] Although ROI could be used correctly for a wide range of investment decisions, there is no need to use this awkward tool. Our defense of ROI is based on a desire to use it as a means of evaluating the performance of investments after acquisition, not so that it may be used to evaluate the desirability of undertaking investments.

THE CASE OF THE RESOURCE FOR THE FUTURE

All measures of performance used in an incorrect manner will tend to lead to incorrect conclusions. There is a necessity to work to improve the measures and to use them intelligently.

Consider the case of a division manager of a timber company who has the opportunity to invest in 500,000 acres of prime timber land. The catch is that the trees on the land are all seedlings and they will not mature for 30 years. It is agreed by the planning group that the land is a good investment. However, the manager's performance is measured

---

[3]See H. Bierman, Jr. and S. Smidt, *The Capital Budgeting Decision*, (New York, The Macmillan Company, 1975, Chapters 1–7). Keith Shwayder makes similar points in "A Proposed Modification to Residual Income—Interest Adjusted Income," *The Accounting Review*, April 1970, pp. 299–307.

using return on investment. The manager knows that the land will increase the denominator now, but it will be 30 years before the numerator is also increased. Since the division manager only has five years to go before retirement, the investment in land is rejected.

There is a temptation to say that this case has an obvious solution, and so it does. The land should be excluded from the investment base in measuring performance unless the value increment is allowed to affect the income. But unless something like this is done, there will be a distortion in the investment performance analysis, and thus distortion in the investment decision-making criteria applied.

In the case of the future resource just described, the problem and the solution are "obvious." Now consider a plant being built with excess capacity to service the expected demand of 1985. Is this performance measurement problem obvious? Is the normal performance measurement scheme capable of taking this situation into consideration? Probably it is not.

THE COMPUTATION OF ROI

It is widely known that straight-line depreciation or accelerated depreciation, except in very well-defined and specific situations, will distort measures of ROI. Also, the ROI that results for each year will differ from the return computed at the time of acquisition, even when the expected results are realized. The suggestion to solve this difficulty is simple to state although the implementation would require innovation. If the return at time of acquisition is correctly computed (that is, a discounted cash flow procedure is used) and if the ROI each year after acquisition is correctly computed, the two measures will be identical for each year of operation, if the events forecasted at the time of the decision actually occur. We would want this to be the situation, and it does happen. To accomplish this objective, depreciation must be defined in a theoretically correct manner, and the computation of depreciation must be consistent with this definition.[4]

---

[4]For a theoretical paper on depreciation that has relevance to this discussion, see "Depreciable Assets—Timing of Expense Recognition," *The Accounting Review*, Harold Bierman, Jr., October 1961.

Define depreciation to be "the decrease in value of the investment during the time period." Although the definition becomes more complex if there are additional investments made during the period, it can be used to compute the income that is used in the ROI calculations if we assume that this complexity does not exist. The following example is used as a vehicle to show that return on investment, when properly calculated, gives at least as much information as the "residual income method," and in fact the two calculations can be reconciled.

EXAMPLE

Assume the net cash flows (and net revenues) associated with an investment costing $3000 at time zero are:

Time	Cash Flow
1	$1300
2	1200
3	1100

The firm uses straight-line depreciation and has a time value of money of 10%. This investment has a yield (rate of return) of 10%.

Table 4.1 shows the income and investments for each of the three years of use.

Table 4.1

Year	Cash Flows or Net Revenues	Depreciation	Income	Investment at the beginning of the Period	ROI (Income divided by investment)
1	1300	1000	300	3000	0.10
2	1200	1000	200	2000	0.10
3	1100	1000	100	1000	0.10

The fact that each year has identical returns on investment equal to the yield of the investment seems to be a coincidence. However, if we inspect Table 4.2, which shows the present value of the investment at four moments in time (V_i is the value at time i), we see that in each period the decrease in value is $1000 (the value of V_3 is zero), and that in this very special situation the use of straight-line depreciation is correct (if the cash flows are different, the depreciation schedule would be different).

Table 4.2

Time	Flows	Period 1 Present Value Factors	Time 0 Present Values	Period 2 Present Value Factors	Time 1 Present Values	Period 3 Present Value Factors	Time 2 Present Values
1	1300	0.9091	1182				
2	1200	0.8264	992	0.9091	1091		
3	1100	0.7513	826	0.8264	909	0.9091	1000
			$V_0 = 3000$		$V_1 = 2000$		$V_2 = 1000$

The present value at time 0 is \$3000, at time 1 \$2000 and at time 2 \$1000.

The procedure illustrated works with any set of cash flows. There need not be distortion in ROI because of the method of depreciation. In this simplified example, the yield of the investment is equal to the firm's time value of money, and the cash flows of each period equal the net revenues. Different assumptions would add to the complexity of the calculations, but these complications can be solved.

A RESIDUAL INCOME METHOD

Some authors suggest the use of the "residual income method." Using the residual income procedure, interest is deducted from income to obtain a residual income. This procedure is acceptable if we properly define income and investment, the correct interest rate is used, and interest is appropriately assigned to time periods.

Unfortunately, the above requirements will not be fulfilled in a manner that will give theoretically sound (and useful) results if one uses conventional accounting. Using the previous example, we illustrate a correct application of the residual income method.

Define income as net revenue less a capital consumption adjustment and the interest cost on the investment and add the implicit interest revenue earned on the investment during the period. The capital consumption is assumed to be equal to the amount paid at acquisition for the expected cash flows of the period and that this is equal to the present value of the cash flows. For period 1 we have

Net Revenues	$1300
Capital consumption $1300 × 0.9091	1182
Income before interest	$118
Interest cost on investment of $1182:	
$1182 × 0.10 = − 118	
Interest revenue on entire	
investment of $3000 × 0.10 = 300	182
Residual income	$300

The residual income of $300 is the same measure as obtained previously as a component of the ROI calculation. However, the ROI calculation also relates the income to the investment and provides a percentage that has meaning to a manager.

Continuing the example for periods 2 and 3 we have:

	Period 2	Period 3
Net Revenues	$1200	$1100
Capital consumption $1200 × 0.8264	992	
$1100 × 0.7513		826
	$208	$274
Interest		
$ 992 × 0.10 + 1091 × 0.10 = −208		
2000 × 0.10 = 200	−8	
$ 826 × 0.10 + 909 × 0.10 + 100 −274		
1000 × 0.10 + 100		−174
Residual income	$200	$100

Again the measures of residual income coincide with the measures of income that were previously obtained. These results will not be consistently obtained unless depreciation is defined as the decrease in value of the investment in computing the return on investment, and second, in computing the residual income, the capital consumption, the interest cost, and the interest revenue all must be defined in a manner consistent with the above example and calculations.

INTEREST ADJUSTED INCOME

Keith Shwayder suggested the use of "interest adjusted income," a modification of residual income, that is in agreement with an allocation of interest cost typified by the previous example. In addition, he defined the interest cost to be the default free rate rather than the more vague time value of money used in the example, or the cost of capital used by other authors.

TIME ADJUSTED REVENUES

Instead of the cash flows and the revenue measures being identical for each period, let us assume that the timing of cash flows and revenue recognition differ (an example would be the receipt of cash advances in payment for a service not yet performed). The cash flow in period 1 of $1300 gives rise to revenues of $1430 in period 2.

Continuing the example, assume that the following facts apply:

	Period			
	1	2	3	4
Cash flows	1300	1200	1100	
Revenues		1430	1320	1210

The revenue used is a sophisticated "time adjusted revenue" measure rather than a naive measure coinciding with the amount of cash received. For example, if $1000 were to be received one year from now but the revenue is to be recognized now, the time adjusted revenue would be $1000 $(1+r)^{-1}$. In like manner, expenses would have to be time adjusted.[5]

Applying the present value factors to the *revenue measures,* we obtain the following values at different points in time and the resulting depreciation.

Time	Value	Depreciation for period
0	3000	
1	3300	− 300
2	2200	1100
3	1100	1100
4	0	1100

The computations of incomes and returns on investment for each period would be

Period	Revenues	Depreciation	Income	Investment	Return on Investment
1	0	− 300	300	3000	0.10
2	1430	1100	330	3300	0.10
3	1320	1100	220	2200	0.10
4	1210	1100	110	1100	0.10

It should be noted that time adjusted revenues and cash flows are very much tied together and that they rigorously define the depreciation (the decrease in value) of a period.

A NON ZERO NET PRESENT VALUE

The example used to this point sets the net present value of the

---

[5]For a more complete explanation of time adjusted revenues and expenses see H. Bierman, Jr., "A Further Study of Depreciation" *The Accounting Review,* April 1966, pp. 271–274.

investment equal to zero, that is, the yield of the investment is equal to the time value factor for the firm. Obviously this will only rarely be the case. We expect most investments to have expected returns in excess of their required return. For example, let us assume that investment costs $2760 instead of $3600. The net present value of investment at time of acquisition is $240, and its yield is 0.15. There are several possible paths we can take. The most straightforward would be to use 0.15 as the rate of discount to compute the depreciation expenses and returns on investment.

Using 0.15 as the rate of discount we obtain

Period	Revenue	Depreciation	Income	Investment	ROI
1	1300	844	416	2760	0.15
2	1200	919	281	1876	0.15
3	1100	957	143	957	0.15

The primary difficulty with this solution is that the time value of money is defined to be 0.10 not 0.15. Thus the values of the investment at each time period are greater than those shown in the table. A second solution is to immediately adjust the value of the investment to $3000, the present value of the benefits, despite the fact that the investment cost only $2760. This procedure would not be acceptable for conventional financial accounting purposes because of the implicit threat of manipulation, but it would be perfectly acceptable for internal managerial purposes. It is a very appealing procedure because it is relatively simple and yet is correct from the standpoint of accounts reflecting values.

The third solution compromises and is a combination of the first two procedures. The value of the investment at time zero is defined to be $3000, but the $240 of value increment is treated as initially unrealized. The $240 is realized through time as the asset is operated. Returning to the example in which the cash flows and revenues were identical, we have for each period:

Time	Value using 0.10	Value using 0.15	Value Differences (remaining un-realized value)	Original Unrealized Income that Should be Recognized during the Period
0	3000	2760	240	
1	2000	1876	124	116
2	1000	957	43	81
3	0	0	0	43

For period 1, excluding the $116 would result in a 10% return on investment. Including the $116 in income and using the investment base of $2760 would result in a ROI of 15%.

INCENTIVE CONSIDERATION

The use of book value based on cost to measure the investment (the denominator in the ROI calculation) or even estimates of price level adjusted cost is subject to severe criticism. There is no reason why a system based on managerial values cannot be used for internal purposes instead of cost based accounting. Here we have an opportunity to apply ingenuity to bypass a valid objection by managers to cost based accounting. Rather than asking an accountant or another staff person to supply the number on which the manager is to be judged, let us ask the manager himself to supply it. The procedure would be simple. Take a set of eligible managers and ask them to "bid" periodically for the assets they want to manage and for which a change in management is appropriate. The bid that is accepted takes the asset, and the bid becomes the accounting base for performance evaluation. If the manager bids too high he gets the asset but will find it hard to meet the return on investment requirements. If he bids too low, he may find that he loses the asset to a competing manager, or alternatively the "board" may reject the bid and ask him to resubmit a bid. There is one major difficulty with this procedure. Managers can rig the time shape of projected earnings so that early targets can be easily attainable. This tendency would have to be controlled by the top managers awarding the bid.

The procedure would have many advantages. It would establish an investment base whose measure is acceptable to both the operating manager and to the top level of management (the former sets the value, the latter must accept it). The accountant serves the very important and proper function of supplying relevant information that is used by the managers in making their respective judgments and bids. The ROI measure is improved because the investment base is appropriate to the specific investment and manager being evaluated rather than being the result of a series of historical accidents (such as the year of purchase and the method of depreciation). Most important, it requires managers to set, describe, and quantify their plans for the utilization of the assets. It would tie together planning, decision making and control.

DEFERRED BENEFITS

Conventional accounting combined with the uses of ROI are at their worst when the benefits produced by the asset are expected to increase through time or when the benefits are deferred. The early years are greatly penalized by conventional accounting, with the manager having incentive to avoid such investments so that his performance evaluation does not suffer.

EXAMPLE

Assume an investment costing $3000 is expected to have the following benefit stream:

Period	Benefits
1	$1100
2	1210
3	1331

The firm's cost of money is 0.10 and equal to the investment's discounted cash flow rate of return. The results using conventional accounting and straight-line depreciation will be (assuming the actual benefits are equal to the expected):

Period	Revenues	Depreciation	Income	Investment	ROI
1	1100	1000	100	3000	0.03
2	1210	1000	210	2000	0.105
3	1331	1000	331	1000	0.331

Defining depreciation expense to be the decrease in value of the asset, the results would be:

Period	Revenues	Depreciation[1]	Income	Investment	ROI
1	1100	800	300	3000	0.10
2	1210	990	220	2200	0.10
3	1331	1210	121	1210	0.10

[1]The depreciation calculations are

$V_0 = 3000$ value at time 0 $d_1 = 3000 - 2200 = 800$ depreciation of period 1
$V_1 = 2200$ value at time 1 $d_2 = 2200 - 1210 = 990$ depreciation of period 2
$V_2 = 1210$ value at time 2 $d_3 = 1210 - 0 = 1210$ depreciation of period 3

The distortion can be increased by assuming no (or very low) benefits until period 3. The results of the early years would appear to be even worse than in the example.

CASH FLOW RETURN ON INVESTMENT

Recognizing the inadequacies of conventional depreciation accounting, some managers have attempted to solve the problems by using cash flow return on investment. Since cash flows are used to evaluate the investment, why not also use them to evaluate the investment's performance?

The cash flow return on investment is defined as

$$\frac{\text{Cash Flow}}{\text{Investment}}$$

Although the computation is appealing because depreciation is not computed, unfortunately, the computation merely makes a bad analysis worse. Using the above example, we would obtain:

Period	Cash Flow	Investment	Cash Flow ROI Cash Flow/Investment
1	1100	3000	0.37
2	1210	2000	0.61
3	1331	1000	1.33

Some firms have actually tried to use the historical measures as required returns for additional investments. You should note that for an investment yielding 0.10 over its life, the cash flow ROIs for the three years are 0.37, 0.61 and 1.33. The measure greatly overstates the ROI the asset is actually earning.

Another difficulty of the measure is that it will tend to bias management in favor of capital intensive methods of production, because capital cost is omitted from the numerator of the performance measure.

It is better to use the conventional ROI with income (after depreciation) in the numerator than to use the cash flow ROI, which is extremely difficult to interpret and has no theoretical foundation. Its use will get management into one or more interpretive difficulties.

PLANNING IMPLICATIONS

The fact that there may be a conflict between the investment criteria used and the performance measures means that corporate planning must take into consideration the fact that all desirable investments (from the corporate standpoint) may not be submitted upward. It would be naive to expect a division manager to recommend a plant with 60% excess capacity where the analysis of mutually exclusive investments indicates that this is the best alternative, if the performance measures for a period of five years will be adversely affected by the choice. Rather the division manager is likely to bury this type of alternative so the board of directors is not confused by the number of alternatives and this "undesirable" alternative specifically.

The board of directors has a similar type of conflict when it evaluates major investments that satisfy normal investment criteria but have adverse effects on the ROIs and earnings per share of the next few years because of conventional accounting.

The planner rejecting investments with positive present values may gain short-run benefits (nondepressed earnings) but will have a long run cost in that future earnings will be depressed compared to what they could have been.

One alternative is to use the recommended investment criteria and hope to modify the accounting conventions that cause the distortions. Alternatively, failing that, management can attempt to explain the characteristics of the investment (and the deferred benefits) to the investing community.

Unfortunately, the accounting profession is more concerned with avoiding excessive optimistic announcements by management than it is with presenting a balanced forecast of the future. As long as this situation exists, and recognizing the fact that even well-intentioned forecast may be wrong, it is not likely that management will want to report present earnings are understated and future earnings will justify an investment that is currently reported as being nonprofitable.

The best solution would be for the accounting profession to encourage a wide range of depreciation methods, if these methods are justified by the economic characteristics of the investment.

IMPLEMENTATION CONSTRAINTS

There are difficulties in applying ROI, but these difficulties also tend to apply to other measures. For example, annual accounting profits can be a poor measure of what has been accomplished during any relatively short period of time. Also, it is often difficult to assign responsibility for a deviation from the profit objective. Many economic events with long-run implications are not recorded by the accountant, all managers should be aware of this limitation.

One should not use any performance measure without considering factors, including those factors not normally appearing in the management information system.

CONCLUSIONS

In many cases the ROI should not be used because it is too difficult to measure either the income or the investment. The measure of ROI can and should be improved. It can then be used to gain an impression of managerial performance. This is necessary if the top management of a firm is to attempt to measure the effectiveness of the utilization of assets controlled by persons at different levels of the firm. The return on investment is a very useful means of accomplishing this, if efforts are made to measure income and investment in theoretically correct ways.

Although performance measurement is a difficult task when exact reliable conclusions are not feasible, it is necessary that all managers evaluate persons for whom they are responsible. As a guide and a indicator, ROI has its uses.

CHAPTER 5

THE NATURE OF DEBT

The fret
Of debt:
Earn cash,
No sweat;
No cash—
Regret
No Tax
Offset.

During 1974, corporations issued $31 billion of bonds and $4 billion of common stock.[1] These amounts are consistent with those of the previous ten years (although the common stock amount was somewhat low in 1974 because of the depressed stock market). The issuance of long-term debt has been consistently at least threefold as large as the issuance of new common stock.

Why have corporations tended to use debt rather than common stock in the post World War II period? The primary reason is closely tied to the level of taxation (high) and the tax structure, which gives an apparent tax advantage to debt. The interest paid to debt holders is a tax deduction; thus the interest acts as a tax shield. With a tax rate of 50%, the effective cost of debt capital to a profitable (tax-paying firm) is cut in half.

A second reason is that debt introduces a leverage effect that is attractive to aggressive managers willing to accept a high level of risk.

Portions of this chapter were published previously *Financial Policy Decisions* by Harold Bierman, Jr. (Macmillan, 1970) and are reprinted here with permission.
[1]Federal Reserve Bulletin, June 1975, p. A 39. Another major source of new capital has been retained earnings.

Although debt is widely used in the United States and its use is increasing, a full appreciation of the use of debt requires that we consider the financial affairs of foreign firms. The 1975 annual report of the Mitsui Shipbuilding and Engineering Co., Ltd., showed a total amount of $1115 million of liabilities and $198 million of stock equity as of the balance sheet date. This is a debt equity ratio of 5.63 to 1, an impressive amount of debt. One must move to banks or finance companies to find an industry in which this amount of debt is used in the United States.

In 1976 the *New York Times* quoted Carl Gerstaker, Chairman of the Board of Dow Chemical Company saying "I love to borrow money. I love to owe money."[2]

Mr. Gerstaker increased the company's debt from $455 million to $1.60 billion in ten years. However, the article pointed out that the company's pretax cash flow in 1975 was $1.4 billion and was 14 times the interest cost of $97 million (one should be careful relating the pretax cash flow to interest cost because it is a strange interest coverage ratio).

This article appeared two weeks after an article in the same paper that described the efforts of Japanese firms to reduce the level of their debt.[3] It also was not far removed from articles describing the bankruptcies of W.T. Grant and Franklin National Bank, where the amounts of debt outstanding played significant roles.

There is nothing like a business downturn after a long period of prosperity to educate a new generation of bank loan officers as to the fact that loans can go bad. The following news article lead is of interest:[4] "ATLANTA—James Lientz's office wall is decorated with a framed collection of stock certificates from some of the sorriest companies around. Each one is a real estate investment trust, and several of them owe Mr. Lientz's employer, Citizens & Southern National Bank, a lot of money that may or may not be repaid."

The April 21, 1976 issue of the *Wall Street Journal* carried a news item that indicated that NJB Prime Investors, a real estate investment trust, tendered $15.9 million face amount of convertible debentures. The

[2]*New York Times,* April 25, 1976.
[3]*New York Times,* April 10, 1976.
[4]Bill Paul, *The Wall Street Journal,* March 12, 1976.

tender offer was for $22 cash per $100 principal amount of debt, without any payment of accrued interest. The terms of the offer were heavily influenced by the banks putting up the funds. The holders of the securities had little choice given the financial situation of NJB Prime Investors.

When Penn Central went bankrupt it owed some $6 billion. The debtors thought their debt was secured by a railroad, but then the railroad assets were absorbed in the reorganization of the United States railways under the Consolidated Rail Corporation. When W.T. Grant went bankrupt it owed over $1 billion. Both of these bankruptcies are still unresolved, but it is clear that creditors will not be completely paid off. If more of the assets had been financed with more stock equity, the rights of the debtholders would have been better preserved and the expected losses much smaller.

In 1974 the Franklin National Bank was declared insolvent. In 1976 the company's bankruptcy trustee was quoted as saying "At this time there appears to be no reasonable probability that stockholders of the company will realize any amount of their holdings following the bankruptcy proceedings."[5] The trustee predicted that the bankruptcy proceedings would take ten more years and that it was not clear how much the creditors would receive.

Debt has risk!

THE BASIC NATURE OF DEBT

Debt has a lower explicit cost than common stock, generally has a fixed maturity, and since the debt holders are senior to stockholders, the issue of debt adds to the risk of the stockholders. The tax deductability of interest cost tends to further reduce the explicit cost of debt.

We define the cost of debt to be the rate of interest that equates all future contractual payments of interest and principal to the holders of the debt. Thus if the debt promises to pay $100 a year interest for 20 years and $1000 at maturity, and the bonds are issued at $1000, we conclude that the cost of the debt is 0.10. If the bonds were issued at a price of $851, we assume that the cost of debt is 0.12, because that is

[5]*Wall Street Journal,* June 2, 1976, p. 12.

the discount rate that equates the sum of the present value of all future payments to $851:

	Contractual Dollar Amounts	Present Value Factors (0.12)	Present Values (using 0.12)
Principal	$1000	0.1037	104
Interest per year	100	7.4694	747
			851

If interest is deductible for taxes in the situation in which the 10% bonds are issued at par, and if the corporate tax rate is 0.4, the after-tax cost of the debt is 0.06. This assumes the presence of taxable income; thus the tax deduction can be used. If the tax deduction cannot be used, the before-tax cost of 0.10 becomes the after-tax cost.

The definition of cost used here is not exact. If we considered uncertainty explicitly, we would recognize that the payment of interest and principal are not certain, that the expected values to be collected are likely to be less than the contractual amounts, and that the investors are not likely to be making their decisions using expected monetary values (there may be an element of risk aversion). Also, if the debt has been outstanding and can be retired at a cost difference than the par value, the cost of the debt is based on the after-tax outlay required to retire the debt. Despite these initial complications, we use the common and simple interpretation of cost of debt that has been described.

SUBORDINATION AND THE COST OF DEBT

Assume that a new firm has assets that have been acquired and financed with common stock, and now it is possible to substitute some debt for common stock. Furthermore, the firm may wish to issue additional debt in the future. This additional debt may or may not be identical to the original debt with respect to its priority in case of bankruptcy. The primary question we consider is how the cost of present and future issues of debt is influenced by the number of different categories of debt used, and by the protection that may or may not be given the holders of a particular category against the possibility that additional debt of an equal or higher priority may be issued in the future.

In practice, the situation is complicated by a number of considerations, including the possibility that the value of the assets securing a particular category of debt will change through time. To simplify the exposition we assume that the assets of the firm are replaced as they wear out, as long as the firm is not bankrupt. There is no likelihood that the quantity of assets owned by the firm will increase.

In this chapter, debt category A is defined to be senior to debt category B if all the claims of A's contract must be fully satisfied before any assets can be applied to satisfy the claims in B's contract. If A is senior to B, we can say B is subordinate to A. We assume (for simplicity) that the only possibilities are that A is senior to B, or A is subordinate to B, or A is equal to B.

A bond category is said to be protected against senior issues if, during the life of the given category, the firm cannot have outstanding a larger quantity of senior debt than was outstanding at the time the given category was issued. Similarly, a bond category is said to be protected against equal issues if, during the life of the given category, the firm cannot issue additional debt that is equal in priority to the given category. If a bond category is protected against both senior and equal issues, the category is described as fully protected. A bond category is said to have limited protection against senior (equal) categories if the firm is allowed to issue a specified amount of additional senior (equal) debt.

Given the assumptions we are making about the possible types of relative priority, there is no logical reason for the potential purchaser of a given category of debt to be concerned about the amount of subordinate debt that is currently outstanding or that may be issued in the future. In the real world, the presence of subordinate debt may cause transaction costs by triggering bankruptcy, thus it is relevant.

In borrowing for the first time, the firm has a number of options available to it that are within the scope of this chapter. First, it must decide the number of debt categories (one or more) to issue simultaneously. Second, it must decide, for each category, whether the category is to be given full protection or only limited protection, and if the latter, how large the limits should be. The firm will be concerned with how these decisions influence the current cost of borrowing and the cost of future borrowing.

COSTS OF SEQUENTIAL ISSUES OF PROTECTED SUBORDINATED DEBT

Suppose that the firm first issued $10 million of fully protected bonds at a cost of 5% and then decided to issue an additional amount of debt. Since the first $10 million of debt is fully protected, the second category of debt must necessarily be subordinate to the first. We can call the first category the senior debt and the second category the junior debt. Suppose the amount of junior debt is $10 million and is fully protected with respect to any issues of debt in the future.

Conceivably some financial analysts might feel that the assets of this company are relatively secure, the risk of default is slight, and that the fact that the second block of debt is subordinated to the first is of minor importance. They might be willing to recommend purchase of this block of junior debt if it were priced to yield slightly more than 5%. It would, however, be inconsistent with the previous assumption to suggest that the junior debt could be priced to yield an amount equal to 5%, since in this case the second block of $10 million is subordinate. If we assume that the average cost of a single $20 million issue of fully protected senior debt would be 6% then the incremental cost of the second $10 million would be 7%.

We would expect many financial analysts to be apprehensive about the security of the assets, and thus be more concerned about the fact that the debt is subordinated. They would be unwilling to recommend purchase unless the junior debt were priced about 7%.

It might be argued that if the firm set out to raise $20 million by debt, two separate issues of $10 million each (one subordinated to the other) might be more or less expensive than one $20 million issue of nonsubordinated debt. The one large issue would be more or less expensive, depending on whether the subordinated $10 million issue would require a quoted yield of more or less than 7%.

We suggest that the cost to the firm will tend to be the same regardless of which choice it makes. In essence, the argument, as it applies to the present problem, is that if the firm issued two blocks of bonds, one subordinate to the other, and both fully protected, an investor could buy a proportion of both blocks of bonds and have the same risk as if the firm had issued one large block, and the investor had invested the same total amount in that block. Assuming that there are some potential investors willing to switch, and that bonds of the same risk class are available as substitutes elsewhere, we expect the average return on the two blocks taken together to be equal to the average return on the large block.

Now assume that potential investors, because of preferences or legal restrictions, are unable to switch from one type of debt to another. The conclusion may still hold that a large issue of nonsubordinated debt will cost the firm the same amount as two separate issues, one senior to the other. Suppose the conclusion were not true, and two separate issues, one subordinate to the other, cost the firm less than a single large issue. Other firms would observe the lower cost and would also issue new debt in the form of separate categories. The firm would refund old debt (in the form of more expensive large blocks) into the less expensive separate issues with different seniorities. Over time the supply of the relatively expensive debt would decrease, and the supply of relatively inexpensive types of debt would increase. This shift would continue until the alternatives of one large issue or several smaller issues (with the different issues having different priorities) were equally expensive.

We conclude that the firm, considering the costs of servicing the debt, should be indifferent as to whether it raises a given amount of debt by making one large issue or several smaller issues, of unequal priority, as long as each issue is protected.

INCOME BONDS

Finance officers are constantly seeking cheaper sources of capital. An income bond is a form of security that has not been used to a large extent, but a discussion of income bonds is particularly useful as a learning device because it helps open our imagination to the possibility of new types of securities. On the spectrum of securities ranked according to riskiness to investors, income bonds would be between subordinated debentures and preferred stock.

In 1955 Sidney M. Robbins wrote a comprehensive article urging a bigger role for income bonds.[6] In a book published in 1966 Robbins and Cohen wrote, "Were it not for the continuing stigma attached to

---

[6]Sidney M. Robbins, "A Bigger Role for Income Bonds," *Harvard Business Review*, November–December 1955.

the income bond as a result of its emergence from railroad reorganizations, it would undoubtedly be used more widely since there is an evident tendency for a corporation's bonds to cost less than its preferred shares."[7]

Income bonds are not easy to define because they come in a variety of forms. They have many characteristics found in regular bonds or preferred stock and thus may be said to be merely variations on bonds or preferred stock. However, if income bonds have essentially the qualities of preferred stock, they would seem to warrant consideration by prospective issuers of securities as a way to avoid income tax; however, if income bonds had the same characteristics as preferred stock there would be no reason to expect special treatment under the tax code as compared to preferred stock. If income bonds are essentially like regular bonds, there would be little reason for using them because they sell at a premium over straight bonds and are not as easily marketable. We attempt to define income bonds so that they find acceptance by both the taxpayer and tax collecter. They are a hybrid combining the characteristics of both their parents; a new variety of security with characteristics that none of the traditional securities capture as well. It is necessary that income bonds be enough like debt so that the deduction of interest on income bonds is included in the government's definition of interest on debt.

CHARACTERISTICS OF INCOME BONDS

Income bonds have a set rate of interest, but the interest must be paid only if earned. The interest may be cumulative to give the investor more security. The interest features of income bonds is different from the dividend features of preferred stock. The most significant difference is that the payment of dividends on preferred stock is more discretionary; it is usually mandatory to pay interest on income bonds if income is earned. The interest payment on an income bond is substantially different from that on straight bonds, since there is no obligation on the part of the corporation to pay interest when it has not earned an

---

[7]Jerome B. Cohen and Sidney M. Robbins, *The Financial Manager* , Harper and Row, New York, 1966, p. 600.

amount equal to the interest. Consequently, income bondholders cannot force a corporation, which has a loss period, into receivership.

Income bonds may give their holders a position preferred to that of general business creditors in the hierarchy of creditor's rights, but below other bondholders. Preferred stockholders are placed below the general business creditors and would be below the income bondholders. The effect of this arrangement, where it exists would make credit a little more difficult to secure with income bonds outstanding than with preferred stock. If the income bonds were made junior to the general business creditors, it would increase the risk of the income bondholders getting nothing in the event of liquidation, but the investors would still be in a better position than the preferred stockholders.

Income bonds must have a maturity date and in this respect differ from the average preferred stock. A maturity date is considered by the tax courts to be a necessary condition for there to be debt (although there is no essential reason for this requirement). If there is a maturity date, there must be some provision for retiring debt. Provision is commonly made in the form of a sinking fund. A maturity date imposes more risk on the borrower. If it does not have the funds for repayment at the maturity date, it may be forced into receivership. Preferred stock has no such risk because no provision must be made for retirement, and there is no way the preferred shareholder can force the issuing firm into bankruptcy. There have been issues of preferred stock with provision for repurchase each year or with provision for mandatory redemption, but these issues are relatively rare.

In summary, income bondholders generally have substantially greater rights against the corporation than holders of preferred stock and fewer rights than bondholders. Income bondholders have the right to demand their money at maturity, and the right to interest if earned. Compared to regular bonds, income bonds are less risky to the corporation because the holders do not have the right to demand interest as it falls due. The risks associated with income bonds are between the risk normally associated with preferred stock and that associated with bonds. What is the optimum mix of securities (from the point of view of the issuing corporation)? A fund raiser can probably get the same degree of risk by using preferred stocks and bonds as it can by using an income bond type security. This may be demonstrated by arbitrarily assigning risk factors of 0 to preferred stock, 1 to income bonds, and 2 to bonds. Risk in the middle ranges may be achieved with or without the use of income bonds. The important question is whether income bonds can be used to achieve given levels of risk more cheaply than combinations of other securities.

USE OF INCOME BONDS

If income bonds can provide a large degree of risk avoidance compared to bonds, why are they not used more? One reason is that income bonds have been used extensively in connection with reorganizations, and thus they tend to be associated with weak corporations. Recently income bonds have been issued by strong corporations, but the historical association with weakness seems to be fading slowly.

A second reason offered is that strong companies do not need to issue income bonds because they can bear the burden of fixed charges on bonds. Although this argument is superficially attractive, it should be noted that even a strong corporation can issue only a limited amount of low-cost debt with low risk. At a given point in time it may be logical for such a corporation to pay the interest premium that income bonds would cost compared to the interest cost of regular debt. Also, the choice may actually be between income bonds and an equity type of security (whose dividends are not deductible for tax purposes).

One fear of financial officers that is preventing the widespread use of income bonds may be that, if many corporations used this type of security to raise capital, the government would react and change the internal revenue code and disallow the deduction. This is a somewhat confused and incomplete analysis. The present code has a bias in favor of fixed-payment type of securities (interest payments being deductible and dividends not). This is undesirable from the point of view of the economy because it leads to corporations being more unstable. Corporations are more susceptible to ruin if business activity slackens. Income bonds used instead of regular debt adds to the surviving power of a corporation rather than reducing it, and as such should be welcomed by government decision makers. The market may have to be educated as to the nature and advantages of income bonds. Perhaps a new title is needed such as "preferred income bonds." In any event, given the present tax code, it is apparent that there is a place in the capital structure of a corporation for income bonds. The corporate financial officer who does not investigate the possibility of their use is giving up the opportunity for tax savings (where the income bonds are used instead of equity-type securities) or reducing risk (where the income bonds are used instead of pure debt).

MEASURING DEBT

Accountants implicitly or explicitly make use of the present value principles in the measurement óf long-term debt. However, they have done so incompletely and inexactly. For example, when the bond is issued, the liability is recorded at the amount received from the creditors; for a bond with a maturity value of $1000, the liability is measured by the amount of cash received. This eliminates the need for the firm to compute explicitly the present value of the future payments. When the effective interest rate is equal to the contractual rate of the debt, the amount received at time of issue is equal to the amount to be paid at maturity, assuming the interest is paid periodically. That is, the cash received is equal to both the maturity amount and the present value of the debt using the current effective interest rate.

An important operational weakness of this practice is that it complicates interfirm comparisons because the debt-type cash flows are implicitly discounted using different discount rates. Consider the following example:

Company A issues $10 million of 20-year 5% bonds at 5%, its effective rate of interest, and the debt is recorded at $10 million. Company X issues $10 million of 20-year 10% bonds at 10%, its effective rate of interest, and its debt is recorded at $10 million.

We argue that, in an important sense, the two companies have different amounts of debt outstanding, and that conventional accounting fails to note this. Company A has promised to pay only $500,000 of interest per year for 20 years; Company X has promised to pay $1 million a year interest for the same period. Both companies have promised to pay $10 million at maturity.

We review (1) the factors that required Company X to promise to pay the larger interest payments in order to receive the same amount of cash as Company A, and (2) the reasons Company X might have been willing to enter into this debt contract.

EXPLAINING DIFFERENCES IN BOND INTEREST RATES

In the example, we assume that both sets of bonds were issued at par and at the same time. Therefore, the difference in the quoted yields (which are equal to the contractual rates in this case) must be due to differences in risk in the two firms and not to differences in general economic conditions.

Since we conclude that the yield differences result mainly from investors' evaluation of and reaction to the risk of default (assuming the bonds have similar call protection and other such contract provisions), we examine how this reaction may lead to the observed differences. Potential investors may not analyze default risk in the exact manner adopted here but the computations are illustrative.

Table 5.1. Present Value Computations Using the Default-Free Rate

Dollar Amounts	Present Value Factors (0.04)	Company A	Company X
$10,000,000	0.4564	$4,564,000	$4,564,000
500,000 per year	13.5903	6,795,000	
1,000,000 per year	13.5903		13,590,000
Present value of the liabilities		$11,359,000	$18,154,000

If there were no risk of default, it would be possible to obtain a reliable predictor of the value of the bonds of Company A and of Company X (and therefore a predictor of how much the companies would obtain by selling them) using the yield on U.S. government bonds of similar maturity. Suppose that when the bonds were issued U.S. government bonds of the same maturity have a 4% yield. The present values of the liabilities of Companies A and X using a 4% interest are computed in Table 5.1. These present values are predictions of the value of the bonds if they were default free. We cannot assume there is no risk of default for the securities of A and X. Investors do not expect to receive the amounts listed above, because they do not consider the bonds to be default free. Although there is no objective means of determining the probabilities of default that investors actually assign, we consider two sets of investors' beliefs about the probability of default. We sacrifice realism in order to simplify the explanations and computations; for example, we assume that investors believe receiving the principal is certain but the interest payments are uncertain.

First assume that investors believe that there is a 0.8 probability of prompt receipt of all the interest payments from Company A's bond, and a 0.2 probability that no interest payments will be made. For Company X, there is a 0.4 probability of receiving and 0.6 probability of not receiving the interest payments. There is probability 1.0 that the principal will be paid in both cases. The expected present values of the cash receipts under these assumptions are given in Table 5.2.

Table 5.2. Computations of Expected Present Values

Amounts	Present Value Factors (0.04)	Present Value	Probability of Present Value	Expected Values Con,pany A	Company X
$10,000,000	0.4564	$4,564,000	1.0	$4,564,000	$4,564,000
500,000	13.5903	6,795,000	0.8	5,436,000	
1,000,000	13.5903	13,590,000	0.4		5,436,000
Expected net present value				$10,000,000	$10,000,000

Table 5.2 illustrates one explanation for the amounts investors were willing to pay for the two bond issues. The bonds were described as having coupon rates (and effective yields) of 5 and 10%. But bond yields are conventionally quoted on the basis of contractual obligations, not investors' expectations. Investors in fixed income securities should expect to receive less than the amount to which they are legally entitled. If the probabilities given in Table 5.2 apply, we could say that investors' expected annual interest receipts for both bond issues were only $400,000 ($500,000 × 0.8 from Company A, and $1 million × 0.4 from Company X).

If we knew that the probabilities given in Table 5.2 were correct, the fact that both sets of bonds sold for $10 million would indicate that investors are willing to buy bonds on the basis of the expected present value of the cash flows.

In this example, the probability of default affects the amount of the expected cash flow; the 20-year bonds of Company A, Company X, and the U.S. government all yield an expected $400,000 per year. The example uses probabilities to compute the expected monetary value, but there is no adjustment for possible risk aversions of investors.

When the discounting process and decision making under uncertainty are better understood we may expect a series of computations similar to the above. These computations may require the accountant to modify or discard old rules and to supply more information. The suggested procedure enables us to evaluate more effectively different debt contracts. The information given by the market value of the debt or, equivalently, by the cash received is less useful than the more complete description of the liability using the present value of the contractual payments adjusted for the possibility of no payment and the risk attitudes of the investors.

THE DEBT OF EXXON

The long-term debt of the Exxon Corporation is shown on the balance sheet of its 1975 annual report at an amount of $3451 million. This amount is a combination of different currencies (translated using the year-end exchange rates) and different interest rates. The contractual interest rates varied from 5.1% to 9.5%, and the maturity dates varied from 1976 to 2005.

The present value of the liability using the current effective interest rate or a default free rate would be different from the reported liability. Although the total liability could also be affected by the omission of the past service liability for pensions, or for leases not reported and capitalized, the primary reported item to be corrected would be a measure of the present value of the long-term liability. The contractual cash flows are known with certainty; only the discount rate is subject to a difference of opinion.

THE DEBT OF CHRYSLER

The debt of Chrysler Corporation is also of interest. As of December 31, 1975 the company showed total liabilities of $3858 million (this was 62% of total assets). This is a large amount of debt but not shocking. However, Chrysler does not consolidate all its subsidiaries, and it has a captive finance company. The investment in Chrysler Finance is shown on the asset side of the parent's balance sheet, but since the financial affairs are not consolidated (this is common practice, and Chrysler is only doing what many other firms do) the liabilities of Chrysler Finance are not shown. These liabilities are $2793 million.

The game does not end here. In addition to Chrysler Finance, there is Chrysler Realty Corporation with $380 million of debt.

And now, the interesting point is to be made. Both Finance and Realty have assets that indicate there are other subsidiaries that have more debt that is not listed. How much more? We do not know.

It is true that these components we have discussed are separate corporations, each with limited liability. However, it is difficult to imagine the parent walking away from the debt of its subsidiaries in a situation where there was financial difficulty.

Whenever there is an asset on a balance sheet of a corporation "Investment in Nonconsolidated Corporations" or some similar title, the reader of the report is being warned that there is likely to be debt outstanding which the parent firm may be responsible for in the future.

New York State issued bonds that could not have been issued under the constitution of the state as full faith and credit bonds. These were only "moral obligations" and not debt of the state. However, when the Urban Development Corporation became insolvent, the state could not turn its back on these moral obligation bonds. They were effectively debt of the state, even though they could not legally have been issued as such.

MUNICIPAL UTILITIES

On April 14, 1976 the *New York Times* carried two tombstones.[8] One was for $60,000,000 of serial First Mortgage Bonds issued by Pennsylvania Electric Company to pay 9% and to come due through the year 2006. The second issue was a $100,000,000 issue of serial bonds maturing as late as year 2019 and paying interest rates ranging from 5% to 6.60% depending on maturity. This second issue was exempt from all federal income taxes and was issued by the Washington Public Power Supply System.

[8]A tombstone is an advertisement announcing the issuance of securities and listing the underwriters.

The Washington issue underlines the expanding role of municipal utilities in the United States. This one system is expected to need $5.2 billion in the next ten years.

The total invested in nonprivate utilities was expected to be over $4 billion in 1976.

The tax exemption of such utilities is a powerful factor encouraging growth. The interest payments are tax exempt, and the properties are also tax exempt. These are incentives for having facilities owned by government entities. Is this a desirable state of affairs?

CONCLUSIONS

In evaluating the cost of borrowing, one must consider both the priority status of a debt issue compared with other existing issues, and the type of protection the debt carries against the possibility of subsequent issues of debt with equal or higher priority.

We doubt that a firm can lower its real cost of borrowing by issuing at the same moment in time debts in many priority categories. Such attempted discrimination can be expected to be effective only if potential lenders are restricted to a narrow range of securities and if a limited group of corporations is able to issue their securities. These limitations are not characteristic of modern capital markets.

By contrast, we believe that whether or not debt issues are protected against future issues can make a difference in the firm's real cost of borrowing. A firm that has a preference for minimizing the maximum interest rate on its debt can achieve this goal by issuing debt carrying no protection or only limited protection to lenders against future issues of the same or higher priority. However, the lower maximum interest rate achieved this way is likely to lead to a higher average real cost of borrowing.

The types of subordination and protection against subsequent issues are only two of the many ways in which a debt issue can be characterized. However, an understanding of how these characteristics affect the cost of debt is necessary to an understanding of the overall cost of raising capital.

We find the tax status of both income distributions and operating entities affecting the type of security to be issued. For example, there is the question of income bonds versus stock as well as the emergence of municipal utilities.

CHAPTER 6

THE USE OF PREFERRED STOCK

> Preferred stock is a fooler.
> Do not try it.
> The only thing "preferred" is that
> You not buy it.
> Its payments are unsure
> And its dividends are set.
> A debenture bond
> Is a better bet.*

In 1974 there was $2.3 billion of preferred stock issued in the United States, compared to $32 billion of long-term debt and $4 billion of common stock.[1] At that time preferred stock yielded 8.23% compared to Baa corporate bonds yielding 9.5% (Aaa bonds were yielding 8.5%).[2] Why did firms issue high interest and risky debt when they could issue relatively low-yielding preferred stock? Why did investors buy preferred stock yielding less than debt when the debt had less risk?

In the long distant past, when taxes were low, preferred stock was a popular method of raising capital. In recent years the use of preferred stock, with few exceptions, has been limited to public utilities and firms engaged in mergers and acquisitions. There is a good reason for the decrease in its use. Its fixed dividend payments are not deductible for income tax purposes, whereas debt interest is deductible. This tends to make preferred stock a high-cost method of raising capital.

Preferred stock is somewhat like debt (a commitment by the corpora-

---

*This advice is for an individual who does not have the dividend received credit that is available to a corporation.

[1]*The Federal Reserve Bulletin,* June 1975, p. A39.

[2]*Ibid.,* p. A28.

tion to pay a well-defined amount) and somewhat like common stock (the amount to be paid is not a fixed legal commitment; although the amount of the dividend is fixed, it does not have to be paid by the corporation). Thus preferred stock falls between debt and common stock on the capital structure spectrum.

It should not be assumed that all preferred stocks are equal. They may differ in respect to conversion into common stock, be cumulative, be callable, be participating, and may be of finite or infinite life.

THE COST OF PREFERRED STOCK

Assuming that the life of the preferred stock is infinite, the cost of the stock is

$$\text{Cost of Preferred Stock} = \frac{\text{Annual Dividend}}{\text{Price}}$$

For example, a stock being issued for $50 and promising to pay $3 a year dividend would have a cost of 0.06; that is,

$$\frac{\text{Annual Dividend}}{\text{Price}} = \frac{3}{50} = 0.06.$$

Note that the par value of the stock does not affect the cost, but the market price and the amount of the promised dividend do affect the cost.

If the company currently has the preferred stock outstanding and it can be repurchased at a cost of $50, the cost of the preferred stock is again 0.06, where the 0.06 is an opportunity cost. By buying a share the company can save $3 of dividends per year.

Now assume that the corporation has a tax rate of 0.40. The before-tax cost to the corporation of the preferred stock is 0.10.

For example, if the corporation raised $50 and earned $5, before tax, the corporate tax would be $2 and the after tax earnings would be $3, just enough to meet the dividend requirement.

If the $50 had been raised by issuing debt paying 0.06, the firm could pay the $3 interest by earning just $3, since the entire $3 is tax shielded.

With a 48% tax rate in 1974, the after-tax cost of Baa debt was 9.5(1−0.48) or 4.94%. Thus the debt had a lower after-tax cost than the 8.23% preferred stock, and the firms raising capital had a clear incentive to issue debt rather than preferred stock. This is reflected in the fact that there was 14 times as much debt as preferred stock issued during 1974.

So far debt seems to have a clear tax advantage compared to preferred stock for the issuing corporation. However, the analysis is complicated by the fact that the investor also has tax considerations that affect the return required by investors. This factor helps explain why corporate investors will buy lower yielding, riskier preferred stock rather than go into debt.

INVESTORS AND THE REQUIRED RETURN

Investing corporations apply an 85% dividend received tax credit to preferred stock dividends. This means that only 15% of the dividends are taxed. This option is meant to minimize the effects of multiple taxation of corporate earnings and is not available to individuals (a $100 dividend exemption does exist, but will be assumed not to affect the analysis that follows), thus the opening verse.

If a firm issues a debt to another corporation, the interest income is taxed at the normal corporate income tax rate.

For example, if there is a 0.4 corporate tax rate and if the corporation issuing the debt earns 0.06 with the invested capital and pays that entire amount as interest, the investing corporation will earn 0.036.

Now, if the corporation issues preferred stock and earns 0.06, it will be able to pay 0.036 of dividends. The corporation buying the preferred stock will pay a tax on 0.15 of the dividends received. The net after tax will be less than that with the issuance of debt. The net return (after tax) of 0.03384 is less with preferred stock than the net return of 0.036 with debt. Even with the 85% dividend received credit tending to enhance stock, debt has a net tax advantage compared to preferred stock. Nevertheless, public utilities continue to issue preferred stock in large quantities because insurance companies like to have some preferred stock in their portfolios. The utilities benefit by the strengthening of their capital structure by the issuance of the preferred stock compared to the issuance of debt.

Taking the information of 1974, a $1000 investment in preferred stock would yield $82.30. For a corporate investor only 15% of $82.30, or $12.35, would be subject to tax. With a 48% tax rate this would be a tax of $5.93, and the corporate investor would net $76.37. Investing in Baa bonds, the same corporate investor would net only $95(1−0.48) = $49.40. Thus the corporate investor would have an incentive with the given yields to purchase some preferred stock despite the lower before-tax yield of preferred stock compared to debt.

As the tax laws currently stand, preferred stock is inferior to bonds as a means of raising capital. A change in the tax laws would change the analysis and the conclusions. For example, if the preferred stock dividend were tax deductable by the issuing corporation, this would make preferred stock more than competitive with debt from the point of view of the issuing corporation.

RISK CONSIDERATIONS

Despite the tax advantage of debt, it can be argued that debt is more risky to the corporation because of the fixed legal commitment to pay interest that is not present with preferred stock. There is an important limitation of the risk argument. First, and most important, the difference between the after-tax cost of interest and preferred stock dividends can be used to retire the debt and thus reduce the risk of the debt. In fact, in a surprisingly short period of time the entire debt issue can be retired with such savings.

If we equate the present value of the annual cash flow savings to the present value of the debt using the after-tax borrowing rate, we find the length of time required to use the savings from the debt to retire the debt.

EXAMPLE

Assume that $10 million of debt costs 0.10, and an equal amount of preferred stock costs 0.09. The corporate tax rate is 0.40. How long would it take to pay off the debt using the after-tax difference in cash outlays?

The after-tax cash outlay of the interest is $1,000,000(1−0.4)= $600,000, and for the preferred stock dividends the outlay is $900,000. The firm can save $300,000 each year in outlay necessary to service the

$10 million of capital assuming it has taxable income.

Let $B(n, r)$ be the present value of a dollar a period for n periods. We want to equate the present value of $300,000 of savings a year to the present value of $10 million using the after-tax borrowing rate of 0.06:

$$300,000\, B(n,\ 0.06) = 10,000,000\, (1.06)^{-n}$$

$$\frac{B(n,\ 0.06)}{(1.06)^{-n}} = 33.3$$

The value of n for which the above equation holds is found by trial and error (a sequence of calculations) to be approximately 19 years.

	$n = 15$	$n = 19$	$n = 20$
$B(n,\ 0.06)$	9.7122	11.1581	11.4699
$(1.06)^{-n}$	0.4173	0.3305	0.3318
$\dfrac{B(n,\ 0.06)}{(1.06)^{-n}}\ =$	23.27	33.76	36.79

In approximately 19 years, the company issuing debt, by buying its own bonds each period with the savings, can retire the entire debt issue. Thus it is difficult to say absolutely that the debt is more risky than preferred stock. If one considers a long-time horizon, one can say that initially the debt is more risky, but as debt is retired, the small amount of debt becomes less risky than a large amount of preferred stock, until finally it becomes obvious that debt is less risky (e.g., there is no debt outstanding).

A second reason why preferred stock cannot be clearly justified over debt based on risk considerations is that, at most, it can be argued that either preferred stock or common stock should be issued. It can be argued that common stock has tax advantages compared to preferred stock. Common stock may lead to capital gains based on superior performance of the corporation. Preferred stock may lead to a capital gain because the discount rates used by the market have fallen, but superior performance by the firm is not apt to significantly affect the market price of the preferred stock because the cash dividend is fixed by the terms of the preferred stock.

The special tax treatment afforded capital gains gives common stock an institutional advantage compared to preferred stock. If it were not for the tax consequences, assuming market forces worked rationally, a firm would not expect to gain an advantage or suffer a disadvantage by issuing preferred stock.

There are several ways the indifference between preferred stock and common stock without taxes can be shown, but only one technique is illustrated.

EXAMPLE

Assume a firm of size $10 million is expected to earn $1 million. If it is financed by common stock, the investors will expect to earn 0.10. If $4 million of preferred stock can be issued at a cost of 0.08, and substituted for $4 million of common stock, the expected return to common stockholders investing $6 million will be:

$$\frac{1,000,000 - 320,000}{6,000,000} = \frac{680,000}{6,000,000} = 0.11\frac{1}{3}.$$

Although the return on investment of the common stockholders has increased from 0.10 to $0.11\frac{1}{3}$, their investment is subject to more risk than if no preferred stock had been issued (the preferred stock investors have prior claim to earnings, although the claim may not be effective).

The investors can adopt a strategy to neutralize the use of preferred stock if they *invest in both common stock and preferred stock* in the following proportions:

$$\text{Percentage investment in common stock} = \frac{\text{Common Stock}}{\text{Total Capital of Firm}} = \frac{6}{10}$$

$$\text{Percentage investment in preferred stock} = \frac{\text{Preferred Stock}}{\text{Total Capital of Firm}} = \frac{4}{10}$$

The expected return of the investors is:

$$0.11\frac{1}{3}\left(\frac{6}{10}\right) + 0.08\left(\frac{4}{10}\right) = 0.068 + 0.032 = 0.10.$$

This is exactly the same expected return they would earn if the firm had been financed completely with common stock.

Actually, the described investment strategy leads to a far stronger result than the same expected return. No matter what the firm earns, the investor will earn the same return with the given investment mix as would have been earned with all common stock financing. For example, if the firm earns $2 million and if it is financed completely by common stock, the stockholders will earn 0.20. If preferred stock is used, the investor following the above strategy for investing in both preferred and common stock will earn:

$$\frac{2,000,000 - 320,000}{6,000,000} \left(\frac{6}{10}\right) + 0.08 \left(\frac{4}{10}\right) = 0.168 + 0.032 = 0.20.$$

Effectively this means that with zero taxes a firm's securities cannot sell at a discount because it is using preferred stock, compared to an identical company using just common stock. If it is selling at a discount, the knowledgable investor can switch from the common stock firm to a mixture of the securities of the preferred stock firm. With taxes, the indifference situation is eliminated because common stock offers tax deferral advantages to the investor.

We have not shown that the preferred stock issuing firm cannot sell at a premium. In fact, this cannot be proven mathematically, but we can guess that more or less the same level of risk and return can be obtained by mixing common stock and debt or by the investor borrowing funds using personal credit; thus it would be very surprising if the preferred stock firm sold at a premium.

MERGERS AND ACQUISITIONS

Preferred stock has been a popular security in mergers and acquisitions when the acquiring firm has felt that it could not issue more debt because of risk considerations, and when the stockholders selling out wanted a somewhat more certain return than could be obtained from common stock (which might be paying a low dividend or not paying a dividend at all). Add a conversion feature to further enhance the preferred stock (the new investors have a chance to share in the benefits if the firm performs in a superior fashion), and stockholders selling out have a chance to participate in any large gains that might occur.

It is in connection with mergers and acquisitions that it is easiest to defend the use of preferred stock. Even then it is difficult to overcome the tax advantages of debt and common stock.

PREFERRED STOCK AND SHORT TERM INVESTMENT

Practically all preferred stock is issued without a maturity date (however, the issue may be callable by the issuing corporation). This infinite life causes the price of the security to be more sensitive to changes in the market discount rate than shorter-lived securities.

If a preferred stock had a maturity date, the short-lived preferred stock would be an interesting security for a corporate treasurer investing short-term funds because of the 85% dividend received credit (although it might still be hard to beat debt with tax-deductible interest). However, as long as preferred stock has an infinite life, a corporate treasurer who likes to sleep at night should not invest short-term money in preferred stock. Small changes in interest rates can cause large changes in value.

PREFERRED STOCK AND CORPORATE FINANCIAL PLANNING

All real-world situations differ from each other, and it is difficult to reach iron-clad generalizations. The logic of this chapter leads to the conclusion that corporations should rarely issue preferred stock. A change in the tax law or other institutional factors (such as a law requiring insurance companies to hold preferred stock) could alter this conclusion, as could a group of investors insisting on recceiving preferred stock in a merger or acquisition.

The right to issue preferred stock gives the corporate financial officer more flexibility in choosing financing alternatives. This flexibility in choosing financing alternatives has value because it might enable the firm to move rapidly in a situation in which preferred stock is the only feasible alternative. Although the long-range financial plan might not include preferred stock, at any moment in time it might be appropriate for a corporation to use preferred stock, because of special circumstances. It is wise for a corporation issuing preferred stock to have that preferred stock callable at the option of the firm. Preferred stock issued today can be very expensive tomorrow if interest rates and required dividends yields were to decrease dramatically.

CHAPTER 7

COMMON STOCK

It may come as a shock
High PE common stock
Is risky. At worst
The bubble may burst.
At best, growth will slow,
But when, we don't know.

The residual ownership of a corporation lies with the common stockholders. The debt and the preferred stock are paid first, and the common stockholders have claim to what is left. Because the common stockholders of a firm are in a more risky position compared to the debt and preferred stock, it is reasonable to expect that they would require a higher expected return than the other capital contributors (however, some investors might accept a smaller return in order to have a chance, no matter how small, of large gains).

The common stockholder of a publicly held firm benefits in two ways from holding common stock. There are the possibilities of receiving cash dividends and obtaining increments in value (price appreciation). The remainder of the chapter is concerned with describing the required return of common stockholders and stock valuation relationships.

THE VALUE OF COMMON STOCK

A share of common stock has value either because of the intrinsic value of the firm in which it represents ownership or because we expect the market to behave in a nonrational manner and to attribute value when there is none. We discard this latter approach, which requires that a "greater fool" exist who is waiting to pay more for a security than it is worth. We assume that a share of common stock has value because of the future dividends that will be paid, and price increases in common stock reflect increased expectations about the future of the company.

We want to define the value of a share of common stock in terms of the future benefits that the common stock will earn for its owner.

Let

P_t be the market price per share at time t (P is the price now)

k be the time discount rate applied by stockholders

g be the growth rate in earnings and dividends

E_t be the earnings per share at time t

b be the retention rate and $(1 - b)$ be the dividend rate

D_t be the dividend at time t where $D_t = (1 - b)E_t$

We can describe the price now of a share of common stock P_0 in terms of the next dividend to be received (assume the dividend is to be received today, and we can use D to designate this dividend) plus the price of the common stock one time period in the future $P1$ discounted back to the present by dividing by $1 + k$.

$$P = D + \frac{P_1}{1 + k} \tag{7.1}$$

This equation states the well-known fact that the price today is equal to the dividend now plus the discounted value of the future price. We can now write P_1 in terms of the next dividend and the price at time 2.

$$P_1 = D_1 + \frac{P_2}{1 + k} \tag{7.2}$$

Substituting $(D_1 + P_2/ (1 + k)$ for P_1 in the first equation we have

$$P = D + \frac{D_1}{1 + k} + \frac{P_2}{(1 + k)^2} \tag{7.3}$$

Continuing this process of substitution, we obtain an infinite series of dividends discounted back to the present.

If we assume that dividends grow at a constant rate g and if g is less than k this infinite series can be summed to obtain the very important stock valuation relationship:

$$P = \frac{D}{k - g}. \tag{7.4}$$

Solving for k we obtain

$$k = \frac{D}{P} + g. \qquad (7.5)$$

We can define k to be the cost of common stock equity. Although k is defined in terms of future dividends, it should be noted that the growth in dividends (g) that is forecasted cannot be independent of the forecasted future incomes. In practice, a forecast of future dividends is apt, to some extent, to be based on past incomes and past dividends.

Note also that the above derivation of k in terms of (D, P, g) assumes that transforming the future price per share (or dividends) back to the present can be accomplished by using a constant k each time period and compounding the term 1 plus k for the number of time periods. With an assumption of certainty, this procedure would be completely acceptable. Relaxing this certainty assumption, it is not clear that investors do, or should, behave in this manner. Nevertheless, the normal interpretation of the required return of common stockholders is consistent with the interpretation implicit in the derivation.

The use of dividends in the relationship just given is confusing to some. They would prefer to see earnings used. Letting E be earnings, b the proportion of the earnings retained, then dividends are $(1 - b)E$, and substituting $(1 - b)E$ for D in equation (7.4):

$$P = \frac{(1 - b)E}{k - g} \qquad (7.6)$$

In equation (7.6) the stock price P is expressed in terms of the earnings and the growth in the earnings as well as the dividend policy that is consistent with the assumed growth rate.

STOCK VALUATION

Let us consider the stock valuation model of equation (7.4). Although we would hesitate to use this specific model in practice (it unrealistically assumes a given growth rate of g that goes on forever), it does supply interesting insights.

The price of a share of stock is defined in terms of the current dividend (D), the required return (k), and the growth rate in dividends (g). A change in any of these amounts will change the value (P) of the share of stock.

For example, let us assume that a share of stock is paying $2 of cash dividends, the stockholders want a 0.15 return, and the expected growth rate in dividends is 0.05. The value of a share is

$$P = \frac{2}{0.15 - 0.05} = \$20.$$

If the growth rate were to increase to 0.14, the stock value would increase to $200:

$$P = \frac{2}{0.15 - 0.14} = \$200.$$

A situation in which the company is actually going to shrink (the dividends have a decay rate) at a rate of 0.10, the value of a share would be:

$$P = \frac{2}{0.15 - (-.10)} = \frac{2}{0.25} = \$4.$$

The next step in the stock valuation analysis would be to assume a growth rate for a period of time and then a shift to a different growth rate after a given number of years. Alternatively, a whole series of growth rates can be assumed.

Despite the unrealism of the stock valuation model of equation (7.4), we can expect it to be used in the future as in the past because of its simplicity and the insights it provides.

THE PRICE EARNINGS MULTIPLIER

The price of a share of common stock divided by the earnings per share is defined to be the P/E ratio of the stock. The P/E ratio is the bane of the modern corporate manager. One company earns a $1.20 per share, and its stock sells at a price of $6 (a P/E of 5). A second company earns exactly the same, and its stock sells at $24 per share (a P/E of 20). Why does this "unfair" state of the world exist?

There are rational reasons why one company will have a P/E of 5, and at the same moment in time a second company will have a P/E of 20 (there are also irrational reasons). To explain P/E ratios, we apply the stock valuation model of equation (7.6). The model assumes a constant growth rate through time, which is a drastically simplified version of the real world. Despite this limitation (which can be modified), the model is very useful for explaining the basic factors affecting the P/E ratio of a company in a rational stock market.

Dividing both sides of equation (7.6) by E, we obtain the ratio of price to earnings:

$$P/E = \frac{(1-b)}{k-g} \tag{7.7}$$

Equation (7.7) shows that the price earnings ratio is equal to the dividend payout rate $(1-b)$ divided by $(k-g)$. The larger the growth rate g, the larger the value of P/E ratio that will be justified for the stock. Although we can use equation (7.7) to compute a ratio of price to earnings that is consistent with the expected growth rate, required return, and dividend policy, the actual price earnings multiplier will be observed in the market.

EXAMPLE

Assume that a firm is retaining 0.4 of its earnings, the investors in common stock require a 0.10 return, and the firm is growing at a rate of 0.07 per year. Substituting in (7.7), we obtain:

$$P/E = \frac{(1-b)}{k-g} = \frac{1-0.4}{0.10-0.07} = \frac{0.6}{0.03} = 20.$$

A P/E of 20 is justified if the growth of 0.07 is expected to continue forever into the future. Now assume that the earnings are expected to decrease to a decay rate of 0.02 in the future (g is negative). We now have a P/E of 5.

$$P/E = \frac{(1-b)}{k-g} = \frac{1-0.4}{0.10-(-0.02)} = \frac{0.6}{0.12} = 5.$$

By changing the assumed growth rate, we are able to explain the two P/E's previously described. Growth rate assumptions make a great deal of difference in setting what a company's ratio of price to earnings should be.

In the real world we can expect the value of k to change through time, reflecting such things as changes in the rate of inflation or the riskiness of a specific firm.

For example, consider the situation in which

$$b = 0.4, k = 0.10, g = 0.07, \text{ and } P/E = 20.$$

Now assume that k changes from 0.10 to 0.19 because of a high rate of inflation and an increase in alternative earning opportunities. Investors now require a 0.19 return per year.

$$P/E = \frac{(1-b)}{k-g} = \frac{1-0.4}{0.19-0.07} = \frac{0.6}{0.12} = 5.$$

If the market believes the model and acts accordingly, the corporate president will see the P/E shrink from 20 to 5 because of an increase in the average return required by investors. The firm's stock price decreases despite the fact that the firm has never been more profitable.

A change in b (b is a decision variable because it is determined by the board of directors) may also affect the P/E multiplier. Assume that the b (the retention rate) and r (the average reinvestment rate) are linked together so that the more that is reinvested the lower the average return, and that $g = rb$ (the relationship is more complex if the firm uses debt):

b	r	$g = rb$
0.4	0.175	0.070
0.7	0.140	0.098

If b is raised from 0.4 to 0.7, r will be 0.14 and $g = rb = 0.14\,(0.7) = 0.098$. With $k = 0.10$, we can expect a P/E of:

$$P/E = \frac{1-b}{k-g} = \frac{1-0.7}{0.10-0.098} = \frac{0.3}{0.002} = 150.$$

When g is very close to k, the P/E will be very sensitive to small changes in g. Before accepting a P/E of 150, we must be willing to accept the assumption that the firm will be able to maintain a growth rate of 0.098. Growth rates of this magnitude are difficult to maintain for long periods of time by very large firms (a 10% growth rate implies doubling in size every seven to eight years). It is important to keep in mind the implicit assumptions of the model.

P/E and the Cost of Equity

Some executives use the reciprocal of the P/E ratio as an estimator of the firm's cost of equity capital:

$$k = \frac{E}{P}$$

The numerator is this year's earnings, and the denominator is the current common stock price. The expression fails to consider reinvested funds and the return they will earn. It fails to consider the growth the investors expect from the firm investing in activities that yield better than normal returns. The ratio can be used as an estimator of the cost of equity capital, if certain conditions are satisfied (e.g. zero growth).

Convertible Securities

Convertible preferred stock and convertible bonds have increased in popularity in recent years, especially as securities issued to facilitate mergers and acquisitions.

Preferred stock and bonds have the virtue of defining a return and a priority of payment. This is reassuring to an investor who desires more security than is available to common stockholders.

However, both the preferred stock dividend provision and the contractual interest rate of debt set upside maximums that are undesirable from the point of view of an investor. Since these investors share in difficulties if the financial affairs of the firm get bad enough, it is not unreasonable for them to want to share in the benefits if the rosy expectations are realized. A feature allowing conversion into common stock offers the possibilities of large gains to the investors in convertible preferred stock and debt, enhancing the desirability of such debt and preferred stock to the investing community. From the point of view of the corporation, a conversion feature reduces the necessary dividend payout with preferred stock and contractual interest payment with debt, and thus may be attractive to the corporation.

The drawback of the conversion feature is that it dilutes the ownership of the current stockholders by enabling fixed-income capital contributors to participate in the upside gains that might develop.

Buying a convertible bond may be viewed as the same as buying a bond with an option to acquire common stock (by converting the debt) or buying common stock with downside protection, since the bond value acts as a type of minimum value. It is, by its nature, a complex security and one that is difficult to value, since it incorporates both bond valuations and common stock valuation. The adding of a conversion feature is an excellent device for muddying up the waters of valuation. A bond that might not have seemed to be desirable because of the risk-return situation might become desirable by incorporating the right to convert to common stock.

In addition to convertible bonds, there are bonds with warrants attached. The advantage of such a security to the investor is that the bond is retained when the common stock is acquired, since the stock is issued in return for the warrant and some additional cash. The advantage to the corporation of a detachable warrant is that the corporation receives cash at the time of exercise (if the warrant is exercised). The disadvantage compared to a convertible bond is that the bond is still outstanding after the warrant is exercised, whereas with conversion the bond has been replaced with common stock.

CONCLUSIONS

The P/E multiplier is an easily computed number that gives a prospective purchaser of a firm's common stock an idea of the relationship between earnings and price of the stock. However, each P/E multiplier implicitly assumes something about the future retention rates, earning opportunities, use of debt, and the required return of stockholders. If these assumptions applied by the market are not realistic, the stock price may be too high or too low.

The value of the required return and the value the market places on future earnings opportunities are not controllable by management, assuming a high level of efficiency. However, management can change the amount of leverage, the amount of funds retained, and by seeking out profitable investments can affect the actual return on investment. In addition, management can generally affect the efficiency with which the assets are employed. Thus management, in a variety of real ways, can affect a firm's P/E multiplier.

Making decisions based on P/E factors is a dangerous type of analysis, because it by-passes all the assumptions that are implicit in a P/E measure (such as the level of risk, earning opportunities, retention rate, etc.). It is important to keep in mind the assumptions implicit in the derivation of the model before making decisions based on the model.

CHAPTER 8

FINANCIAL AND OPERATING LEVERAGE

Debt is like a scissor and beware you don't get pinched.
It accentuates the profit or the loss.
In good times it is good, but in bad times it is bad.
Misjudge results and stockholders are cross.

What do a fully automatic lathe and a debenture have in common? Why is a modern steelmill like a mortgage bond? The answer to both these questions is that they add to the leverage of the firm. The lathe and the steelmill affect operating leverage. The debenture and the mortgage bond affect financial leverage. It is argued in this chapter that leverage is a concept and that it does not make a basic difference to stockholders whether the leverage is caused by a real asset or the type of financing used.

The more operating leverage there is, the more a slight swing in sales will cause a wide swing in earnings before interest and taxes. In like manner, the more financial leverage there is, the more a slight swing in earnings before interest will cause a wide swing in income after interest.

In 1973 Chrysler Corporation earned $266 million; in 1974 it lost $41 million, and in 1975 it lost $260 million. This is a highly levered firm both from the point of view of financial leverage as well as operating leverage. The fact that the profits swung a total of $526 million in two years illustrates the combined leverage effects. As of 1975 the company not only had a large amount of debt on the balance sheet (2.5 billion) compared to the stockholders equity (2.4 billion), but the off-balance sheet debt was also large. As described in Chapter 5, Chrysler Financial Corporation and several subsidiaries are not consolidated with the parent company, with the result that a large amount of debt is not reported as debt on the balance sheet of the Chrysler Corporation. This large amount of debt interacts with operating characteristics that reflect the large amount of fixed costs of an automobile corporation. A relatively small change in units sold results in a very large change in the net income of the corporation.

OPERATING LEVERAGE

Operating leverage may be illustrated using the familiar break-even analysis. Figure 8.1 shows the total expenses and total revenues for different levels of sales. Revenue and variable costs are constant per unit; fixed costs of F are incurred each period. Figure 8.2 shows the same economic situation, but only the income (the revenues less the total expenses) is shown. The break-even sales is $0Q$ units.

The slope of the earnings before interest and taxes (EBIT) line indicates the sensitivity of income to changes in sales. If we identify Figure 8.2 as reflecting the production-revenue possibilities of firm A and then add comparable information about firm B, we have the situation shown in Figure 8.3.

Figure 8.3 shows that both firms have the same break-even amount of sales (both income lines pass through the point Q). However, with Q_1 sales, B has approximately twice as much income, and with zero sales its loss is about twice as large as that of A.

Operating leverage is obtained in general by substituting fixed-cost facilities for variable costs. The reduction of variable costs tends to increase the incremental profit associated with additional sales, increasing the slope of the income line.

If the firms in Figure 8.3 were producing the same product under different technologies, the B method of operation is preferred to the A method if sales exceed Q. If sales are less than Q, the A method is preferred.

FINANCIAL LEVERAGE

A firm may be said to be levered when there are securities of owner-

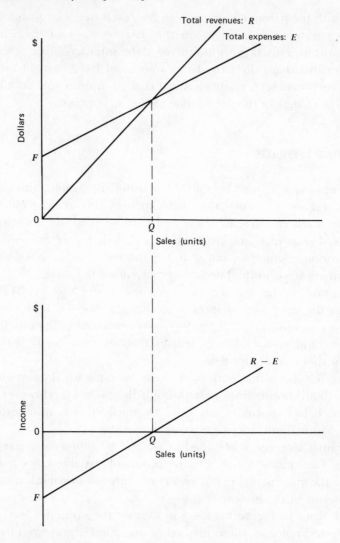

Figure 8.1, 8.2. Break-even analysis: two presentations.

ship outstanding, which have different priorities of payment, and when some of the promised payments for the use of unfunds are of limited amount (so that if more than the limited amount is earned, the holder of a different type of security benefits). Bonds and preferred stock are the securities commonly used to attain leverage for the common stockholders. In this chapter, we deal only with the use of bonds as a form of leverage.

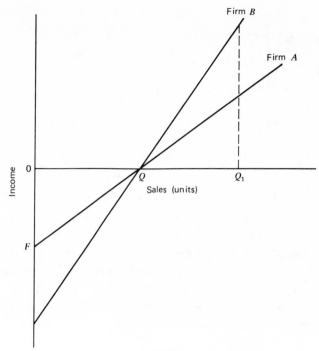

Figure 8.3.   Comparing operating leverages.

The Measurement of Financial Leverage

We want to measure the amount of leverage, since we associate lever-age both with the risk and the opportunities for profit.[1] The measure of leverage is an important input into our evaluation of the value of common stock and also the value of debt.

We define financial leverage as the use of debt in the capital struc-ture. The measurement of the amount of financial leverage is not exact. There are many ways of measuring the amount of leverage, and they may not give consistent measures comparing different firms. However, with any reasonable measure, the addition of more debt will lead to an increase in the measure of leverage. We briefly consider the following measures of leverage:

---

[1]For an interesting and reasonably complete discussion of leverage see J.K.S. Ghandi, "On the Measurement of Leverage" *The Journal of Finance* December 1966, pp. 715–776.

1. Static: book values

2. Static: market values

3. Flows: interest and income

4. Flows: cash flows

Static: Book Values

A conventional measure of leverage is:

$$\frac{\text{debt}}{\text{total capital}} \quad \text{or} \quad \frac{\text{debt}}{\text{stock plus debt}} \qquad (8.1)$$

where all the inputs are book values (a variation is to have "stock" in the denominator rather than total capital).

The advantage of this calculation is that the inputs are very easily arrived at, and the computations are well understood by management. The disadvantage of the procedure is that it uses book values, and the book values may not be relevant measures of the values of the debt or common stock.

Static: Market Values

Although deficiencies in the book measure might lead one to adjust the book values based on available information, in practice, book values are frequently discarded, and the market values of debt and common stock are substituted. This procedure has the advantage of leaving behind the sunk costs and possibly deficient accounting procedures and uses the market's collective judgments of value.

The deficiency of the procedure is that it uses market measures that are, to some extent, based on financial analysis to perform the financial analysis. An alternative to the use of the static measures (either book value or market value) is the use of the several flow measures.

Flows: Interest and Income

One of the most important measures of leverage is the income interest coverage ratio:

$$\frac{\text{income (before interest and taxes)}}{\text{interest}} \qquad (8.2)$$

This is sometimes called the "times interest earned" measure. It relates the net inflow into the firm compared to the debt payment requirements identified as interest. Calculations are made including and excluding tax effects and interest deductions.

This measure has the advantage of being reasonably well defined and easily computed. It is widely used and is probably the best single measure of the impact of the debt on the riskiness of the firm. A low ratio (say less than 2) indicates that a slight downward shift in income will cause the firm to approach the point at which it will not be able to pay the interest on the debt.

Cash Flows

The income interest coverage ratio described above has two difficulties. First, it requires a measure of income, and second, it omits other types of debt payments than interest. The cash flow coverage ratio corrects both of these deficiencies:

$$\frac{\text{Cash in}}{\text{Cash out in payment of debt}} \tag{8.3}$$

The numerator is a measure of the cash flows coming into the firm (essentially the income plus depreciation and other noncash utilizing expenses). The denominator measures the interest, debt retirement, and lease payments. Thus the cash flow coverage ratio is a broader measure of debt obligations than the income interest coverage ratio.

One deficiency of this measure is that it is "near-sighted," and unless it is computed for a series of years extending into the future, significant debt retirement payments could be omitted from the computation (thus leading to an understatement of the amount of leverage).

In addition to computing static and flow measures, we can also combine the two types of measures. For example, the present value of the debt can be related to the net cash flows from operations:

$$\frac{\text{Present value of debt}}{\text{Cash flows from operations}} \tag{8.4}$$

to obtain the "number of years of debt," assuming the cash flows are on an annual basis. Variations of this computation deduct the current assets from the total debt of the firm to obtain a "debt net of current assets" measure (alternatively, the liquid disposable assets can be deducted). This measure has the advantage of combining what is happening to the firm (its flows) and the information about its current financial position.

Which Measure is Relevant?

To some extent, all the above measures are relevant. If the investing public uses a measure to evaluate the value of the firm's securities, that measure becomes relevant to the financial decision maker. If we start with a given financial structure, all the above measures will show an increase in leverage if debt is substituted for common stock. Although the measures may not be reliable in comparing different firms, still, if the cash flow from operations divided into the present value of debt for one firm is 0.6 (say it has $6 million of debt and $10 million of cash flows) and 4.5 for a second firm (say it has $45 million of debt and again $10 million of cash flows), then, unless some facts are introduced, we can strongly suspect that the second firm has more leverage.

Leverage and Risk

The addition of a dollar of debt adds risk to the common stockholders. As the number of dollars of debt increased, the amount of risk to the stockholders is increased. This increase in risk is inevitable, although it is possible to conclude mistakenly that the amount of risk is still so small that for "practical purposes" one can ignore the effect on the stockholders. In the same manner that one more straw may cause a camel difficulties, one more dollar of debt can cause a corporation to have difficulties.

We can describe the effect of adding debt as increasing the variance of the outcomes for the common stockholders. The variance is a statistical measure of the spread of outcomes. The following example is given to illustrate the fact that with zero debt the outcomes to the stockholder are relatively narrow (either $4 or $0 per share), but when a large amount of debt is substituted for the common stock, the range of outcomes increases to either $32.80 or a loss of $7.20 per share. This increase in the spread of the outcomes occurs with the substitution of debt for common stock and is an inevitable result of that substitution.

EXAMPLE

Assume that earnings before interest can be either $4 million with 0.25 probability or $0 with 0.75 probability. The expected earnings are $1 million. The following facts apply:

Capital Structure Alternatives

Stock	Debt	Number of Shares
10,000,000	0	1,000,000
5,000,000	5,000,000	500,000
1,000,000	9,000,000	100,000

Assuming a 0.10 rate of interest, we obtain the following results for the two outcomes.

Different Capital Structures

		Zero Debt		$5 million Debt		$9 million Debt	
Outcome	Probability	Earnings	EPS	Earnings	EPS	Earnings	EPS
$4,000,000	0.25	$4,000,000	$4	$3,600,000	$7.20	$3,280,000	$32.80
0	0.75	0	0	−400,000	−0.80	−720,000	−7.20

The variance of EPS with zero debt is 3; with 50% debt it is 12, and with 90% debt it is 300. An inspection of the table shows that the addition of debt increases the variability of the outcomes. The computation of the variances would lend an exactness to the amount of the increase.

Figure 8.4 shows two curves. One shows total earnings to stockholders through time with zero debt, and the second shows the same earnings assuming that there is debt outstanding. The debt curve remains below the zero line longer. The effect of debt is shown even more clearly in Figure 8.5, which shows the EPS through time with and without debt. The earnings of the "with debt" curve reach greater heights, and the curve stays below the zero line longer.

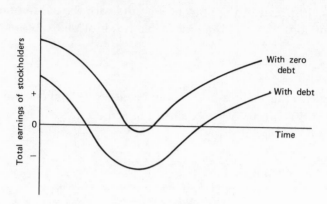

Figure 8.4.   Total earnings with and without debt.

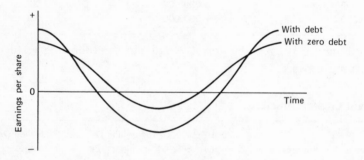

Figure 8.5.   Earnings per share with and without debt.

There should be a clear understanding of the risk consequences to the firm of adding debt. Although we show in the next chapter that it is possible for the individual investor to adopt an investment strategy that will reduce risk, the fact remains that generally debt does add to the overall risk of the corporate entity. Planning requires that management consider the long-term consequences of decisions. The consequence of adding debt is to increase the variability of the return per dollar of common stock investment.

FINANCIAL LEVERAGE AND EARNINGS PER SHARE

Let us assume that a new firm wants to raise $35 million of new capital.

It can use either common stock or a mixture of common stock and debt.

Although it would be incorrect to suggest that one could only look at earnings per share (EPS) data to evaluate debt versus common stock alternatives, since the risks to the stockholders are not held constant, managers are greatly interested in how the EPS is affected. We need a method of determining the amount of earnings before interest necessary for the firm to be indifferent between debt and common stock. Second, for any given earnings before interest and taxes, do we prefer debt or common stock?

We consider different capital structures and the effect of different earnings before interest and taxes on the earnings per share of the firm. Suppose the stock could be issued at $25 per share, and the debt costs 0.08. The tax rate is 0.40.

To raise the $35 million of capital using only common stock would require 1.4 million shares of common stock. However, if 50% of the capital is debt, only 0.7 million shares will be required.

Should the firm issue debt or common stock? Assume that the board of directors wants to know the effect on earnings per share of different capital structures.

Although a table could be prepared showing pro forma income statements for different capital structures, the information that the board needs can be summarized best by means of a graph.

Figure 8.6 shows the relationship between earnings before interest and taxes and earnings per share for the two different types of financial arrangements.

The intersection of the two lines plotted in Figure 8.6 is important. For *any* amount of debt with the same interest rate, the graph of EPS will pass through that same point. If the earnings were known to be $2,800,000, the firm would be indifferent to all possible capital structures, since the EPS will be $1.20 regardless of the structure. The EPS is independent of the capital structure chosen if before interest earnings equal $2,800,000.

The indifference point can be determined graphically as in Figure 8.6 or solved algebraically (the interest rate times the amount of capital gives the indifference earnings).

If the earnings before interest and taxes are expected (are known?) to be larger than $2,800,000, the more debt in the capital structure the better. If the earnings are expected to be less than $2,800,000, an

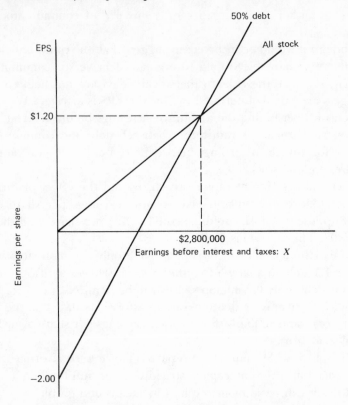

Figure 8.6.   Comparing capital structures: size of firm = $35 million.

all-common-stock capital structure is to be preferred. If the earnings are unknown, the board should be aware that the choice of financing methods is contingent on the probabilities of different earnings taking place and the risk preferences of the decision makers. Financial managers will generally not know their firms' future earnings; thus the value of X that will occur is uncertain. If uncertainty is acknowledged, the analysis being illustrated is a technique that is helpful in understanding the consequences of the decision alternatives, rather than a procedure for clearly defining the right decision.

Raising New Capital

The example assumed that the capital was to be raised by a newly formed firm. We assume the same facts, except that an existing firm is now going to raise $10 million of new capital. In addition, assume that the current capital structure consists of 1.4 million shares of common stock and no debt. Debt will again cost 0.08, and 400,000 shares of common stock could be issued at a price of $25 per share.

Figure 8.7 shows three different alternative financial arrangements. Note that all three lines pass through one point. For any amount of debt paying 0.08, if the earnings before interest and taxes are

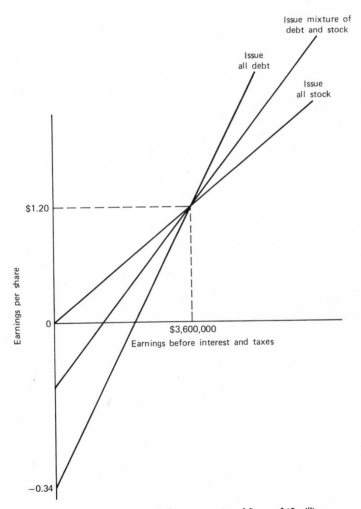

Figure 8.7. Comparing capital structures: size of firm = $45 million.

$3,600,000, the EPS will be $1.20. If the earnings are expected (are known?) to be larger than $3,600,000, the more debt the better. If the earnings are expected to be less than $3,600,000, an all-stock capital structure is to be preferred.

COMBINING OPERATING AND FINANCIAL LEVERAGE

Up to now we have considered operating and financial leverage separately. Figure 8.8 shows a combination of the two types of leverage. It can be seen that a change in the slope in either curve will change the earnings per share of the stockholders that will result from a given amount of sales.

Figure 8.8 shows that if there is Q_1 of sales, the firm will earn X_1 of earnings and r_1 of return on investment.

In this section, we considered the effect of operating and financial leverage on the return to the common stock investors if there are different possible values of earnings before interest before taxes. We did not consider the effect of more debt on the cost of common stock or on the cost of debt (or equivalently on the value of the firm). The fact that beyond some degree of financial leverage (given a constant operating leverage) the cost of debt rises is an added complexity.

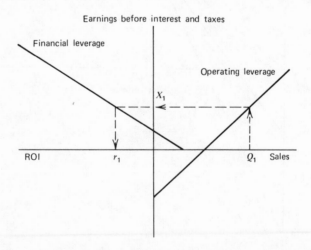

Figure 8.8.   Financial leverage combined with operating leverage.

Planning Considerations

There are companies that will not use debt because it is too risky, and there are companies that will use a lot of debt but will not undertake a real investment with any risk. This chapter attempts to point out that both operating and financial leverage add to the amount of risk faced by investors, and that one should consider the overall risk to the firm. The planner should attempt to optimize jointly the amount of operating leverage (or product risk) and the amount of financial leverage. The Polaroid Corporation has minimized the use of debt because of the inherent product risks it faces when it introduces new products.

The sensitivity of profitability to changes in sales depends both on the amount of operating leverage and the amount of financial leverage. Thus the planner must understand the inherent risk of the product (the fluctuation in sales), the economies of sales and production (the fixed costs and profit margin), as well as the amount of stock equity and debt under the several alternative financing plans. The analyses of this chapter help explain a number of phenomena observed in the business world, such as the extensive use of inventory backlog in industries with high operating leverage and the severe decline in the earnings per share of many firms in the 1975 recession that had earlier demonstrated substantial EPS growth with the help of increasingly greater financial leverage and modest increases in sales.

We leave this risk problem not quite solved. We have suggested that, in addition to the sensitivity of income and return on investment, we must know something about the expected values that result from different decision combinations. One other factor has not been included because the necessary tools have not yet been introduced. We should know how operating and financial leverage affects the way in which the firm's common stock is correlated with the overall market basket of securities. Although the mathematics for this calculation are beyond the scope of this book, one should appreciate that increased operating leverage and increased financial leverage both have the effect of increasing the swings of a specific firm relative to the swings in the market.

CHAPTER 9

CAPITAL STRUCTURE

When financing an asset consider the tax.
Corporate? Personal? These are prime facts.
Draw the graph. You'll see three views,
*But the loopy curve is the one to use.**

CAPITAL STRUCTURE

The financial officers who have conscientiously deciphered the academic literature to determine what decisions should be made relative to capital structure (the mixture of debt and common stock financing) would have had an interesting time over the past 15 years. They would have begun by concluding that there was an optimum capital structure (the so-called classical position). In 1958 they would have been rocked out of their complacency by the classic Miller-Modigliani 1958 article, which informed them that the value of a firm was invariant to capital structure decisions.[1] They would have been somewhat confused by later modifications of the M-M position that indicated that in the presence of corporate income taxes a firm should have as close to 100%

---

*See Figure 9.1.

[1] See Franco Modigliani and Merton H. Miller. "The Cost of Capital, Corporation Finance, and the Theory of Investment," *The American Economic Review*, June 1958, pp. 261−297; "The Cost of Capital, Corporation Finance, and the Theory of Investment: Reply," *The American Economic Review*, September 1959, pp. 655−669; and "Taxes and the Cost of Capital: A Correction," *The American Economic Review*, June 1963, pp. 433−443. Also David Durand, "The Cost of Capital, Corporation Finance, and the Theory of Investment: Comment," *The American Economic Review* September 1959, pp. 640−654; and Alexander Barges, *The Effect of Capital Structure on the Cost of Capital*, The Ford Foundation Doctoral Dissertation Series. Prentice-Hall, Englewood Cliffs, N.J., 1963.

debt as it can achieve. Finally, just as the assumptions behind this latter recommendation were being understood, current theoretical finance literature is suggesting that perhaps the optimum capital structure is somewhere between 0 and 100% debt. Figure 9.1 shows these different alternatives.

The financial officers of a firm are likely to be asked three questions involving capital structure:

1. How is the overall cost of capital of the firm changed by decisions affecting tbe capital structure?
2. How will the firm's value be affected?
3. What is the firm's cost of capital and what is its relevance to investment decisions?

Answers to the first two questions influence the types of securities that

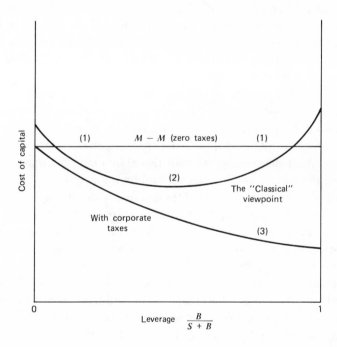

Figure 9.1. Cost of capital.

are issued to investors to finance expansion. The answer to the third question conventionally becomes the cut-off rate (or the rate of discount) for investments. The answers to these questions are not obvious, and it is likely that a person reading the literature pertaining to these questions will become confused.

Definition of Cost of Capital

We define the cost of capital as the cost to the corporation of obtaining funds or, equivalently, as the average return that an investor in a corporation expects after having invested proportionately in all the securities of the corporation. To simplify the discussion, assume that the rates at which the corporation can borrow and lend funds are equal. The definition is appealingly simple and leads to simple decision rules. If the average cost of obtaining funds is 0.10 and if the corporation has an investment that yields more than 0.10, it should accept the investment. Unfortunately, the decision rule and the definition of cost of capital both gloss over considerations of uncertainty and risk preferences that we cannot ignore if we expect the decision rule to be operational in the real world.

Let us define the value of a firm as equal to the present value of all the cash distributed to all capital contributors. Initially we assume that there is no debt outstanding, no taxes, and the firm is not growing. If the rate of discount used in computing the present value can be decreased without decreasing the cash flows, by manipulating the capital structure, the total value of the firm will be increased.

Since the famous Miller and Modigliani article on capital structure and the cost of capital in 1958, a continuing controversy has raged about the sensitivity of the cost of capital of a firm to changes in its capital structure. The controversy is of importance to financial officers, since the effect of capital structure on the cost of capital affects the debt versus common stock decision and the determination of the cost of capital affects the cut-off rate that is conventionally used to determine which independent investments are acceptable. In addition, with income taxes, the capital structure affects the cash flows available for investors.

The broad assumptions made by the several parties to the discussions are worthy of review. The capital structure debate implicitly assumes that

1. There is a definable something that we can label "cost of capital."
2. It is possible to compute the cost of capital with reasonable exactness and meaningfulness.
3. The cost of stock equity capital is the factor used (either explicitly or implicitly) by an investor in common stock in making his investment decisions.
4. Different risk classes of firms have different costs of capital.
5. We can take the cost of capital and use it in making investment decisions. Using the present value method of making investment decisions, it is the rate of discount to be used in choosing the best of a set of mutually exclusive investments, and it is the cut-off rate for accepting or rejecting independent investments.

These assumptions are convenient because they enable a firm to implement the very logical present value procedure, which works in excellent fashion as long as we do not ration capital or allow uncertainty.

Although assumption 1 may be satisfied, there is no reason for assuming that the other four assumptions hold under conditions of uncertainty. No one has shown in a logical manner that the cost of capital can be generally and effectively used in evaluating investments, if the factor of uncertainty is taken into consideration. In this chapter we attempt to determine the effect of leverage on the cost of capital and on the value of the firm, but do not attempt to determine the exact rate of discount to be used in investment evaluation. In Chapter 14 we argue that the use of cost of capital to evaluate investments is not correct.

CAPITAL STRUCTURE AND FINANCIAL ARBITRAGE

Modigliani and Miller, in their 1958 article, stated that "the average cost of capital to any firm is completely independent of its capital structure."[2] If this were not true, "an investor could buy and sell stocks and bonds in such a way as to exchange one income stream for another stream, identical in all relevant respects but selling at a lower price."[3]

Modigliani and Miller illustrated the "arbitrage" process by borrowing on personal account to obtain an equivalent amount of leverage as that obtained by owning a highly levered firm. They also discussed the possibility of "undoing" leverage of a firm by the investor buying stock and bonds. The object of this section is to explore in some detail these two methods of attaining equivalency and to define the necessary conditions for being able to do so. We see that it is not always easy (and sometimes not possible) to obtain equivalency. We define equivalency as being a situation in which the alternatives considered lead to probability distributions of earnings that are identical (the random variables are identically distributed).

We consider two different methods of devising equivalent investment situations:

1. Buying both the bonds and stock of one firm to obtain the same characteristics as buying the stock of a second less levered firm.
2. Borrowing on one's personal account.[4]

Several assumptions are made that run throughout this section:

1. There are no transaction and information costs (it costs the same to supervise two investments as one).
2. There are no taxes.
3. Limited liability does not exist.
4. Financial ruin and resulting transaction costs are not relevant.

---

[2]F. Modigliani and M. H. Miller, "The Cost of Capital, Corporation Finance, and The Theory of Investment," *The American Economic Review,* June 1958, pp. 268–269.
[3]*Ibid.*, p. 269.
[4]We could also show that it is possible to invest in the common stock of two or more firms to obtain the same characteristics as those of a single firm, but we only need the two methods to be described to accomplish the delevering or levering of a firm.

DELEVERING A FIRM

Hedging by Buying Stocks and Bonds of a Firm

An investor can delever a firm by splitting the investment between the common stock and debt of the firm. If the investor buys 0.01 of the firm, the investor buys 0.01 of the common stock and 0.01 of the debt to delever the firm.

EXAMPLE

Let the size of the firm be $10 million with $6 million of common stock and $4 million of debt. The investor has $100,000; thus 0.01 of the firm can be purchased. The debt pays 0.08.

To delever the firm the investor should buy $60,000 of common stock and $40,000 of debt, where these amounts are 0.01 of the outstanding securities:

$$0.01 \ (6,000,000) \ = \ 60,000$$
$$0.01 \ (4,000,000) \ = \ 40,000$$

The investor delevering the firm will earn the same return as if the company were financed entirely with common stock. Table 9.1 illustrates different possible earnings (EBIT) and different capital structures. Note that the earnings with all common stock are identically equal to the total earnings with 40% debt for each of the four possible earning levels.

Table 9.1. Earnings to Delevered Investor

Earnings (EBIT)	Earnings after Interest	Capital Structure: All CS Earnings	Capital Structure: With Debt		
			CS Earnings	Debt Interest	Total Earnings
0	−320,000	0	−3200	+3200	0
100,000	−220,000	1,000	−2200	+3200	1,000
500,000	+180,000	5,000	1800	+3200	5,000
1,000,000	+680,000	10,000	6800	+3200	10,000

The total interest on the \$4 million debt is \$320,000. The investor has claim to 0.01 of this amount or \$3200 interest. We are assuming that interest cost is incurred even if it is not earned (more complex assumptions can be incorporated).

If the earnings of the firm are X and the earnings of the bondholders are I, than we have for an investor owning p of the stock and p of the bonds of the firm:

$p(X-I) = pX - pI$ the earnings of the p proportions of the stock

$\underline{\qquad pI \qquad}$ the earnings of the p proportion of the debt

pX the earnings of the investor who owns p of the firm in total

The investor has the same earnings as would be earned if the firm were fully financed by stock and the investor owned p fraction of the stock. The conclusion is that a levered firm cannot sell at a discount compared to a pure stock firm. If a levered firm is selling at a discount, an investor can sell the stock of an unlevered firm, buy the stock and bonds of the levered firm selling at a discount, and be better off than holding the unlevered firm. Too much debt should not scare investors, since they can delever the firm.

Can a levered firm sell at a premium compared to an unlevered firm? Not if personal borrowing is available at the same cost as the corporation can borrow. It can be shown that an investor can use personal borrowing combined with investment in a lightly levered firm to be equivalent to an investment in a highly levered firm.

The weighted average cost of capital curve is unaffected by capital structure decisions (curve 1 of Figure 9.1), unlike the classical view that there is an optimum capital structure (curve 2 of Figure 9.1). A third point of view discussed in the next section is that the use of debt decreases the cost of capital (curve 3 of Figure 9.1).

These models have several limitations. It is assumed that the firms and the investor have the same borrowing rates despite the fact that the two firms have different amounts of debt, and an individual may have a different risk situation. Just as the same "commodities" cannot sell for different prices in the same market, different "commodities" must sell for different prices. In this case, different amounts of debt are different commodities. If the interest rates for the firms are different, the models become much more complex, and it is necessary that special conditions be filled.

Second, the limited liability characteristic of a corporation enhances having the corporation do the borrowing rather than the individual. Finally, there may be different transaction costs associated with the different strategies.

Since the publication of the 1958 Modigliani and Miller article, the terms "arbitrage" and "homemade leverage" have been widely used in the context of corporation finance. This section attempts to describe the several ways in which arbitrage can be accomplished. However, if we require that interest rates paid by a firm be a function of leverage (all the interest rates not equal), predicting the consequences of attempting to duplicate the leverage of a firm is nontrivial, and the necessary conditions for such duplication are difficult to establish.

CAPITAL STRUCTURE AND THE COST OF CAPITAL

Optimal Capital Structure: Corporate Income Taxes

We have argued that without income taxes the value of a firm could be independent of its capital structure. With corporate income taxes the value of a firm is greatly affected by the fact that interest is deductible for tax purposes and dividends are not. In this section we assume the investors have zero personal tax rates.

EXAMPLE

A firm is considering a $2000 investment earning $100. Debt is available at a cost of 0.05 per year. There is a 0.4 marginal tax rate. With different financing arrangements, the results would be as follows:

	100% Stock	50% Stock 50% Debt	100% Debt
Earnings before tax	100	100	100
less: interest	—	50	100
Taxable income	100	50	0
Income tax	40	20	0
Income after tax	60	30	0
plus: interest	0	50	100
Total contributions to capital	60	80	100

There is a larger after-tax distribution with 100% debt than with any other financial arrangement. If the stockholders buy the debt, there is no additional risk to the stockholders compared with raising the required capital using common stock. Since the total payoff to the capital contributors can be increased by using more debt, the value of the firm can also be increased. In reaching this conclusion, there is an implicit assumption that the capital structures will not be changed in the immediate future.

The question about whether the overall cost of capital of a firm is changed by decisions affecting its capital structure is answered with a yes. If it were not for the income tax laws the answer would be different. The present tax laws, allowing interest on debt but not dividends on stock to be deducted in computing taxable income, results in a clear bias in favor of issuing debt. The reason for this bias is most easily seen where the debt is issued to the common stockholders. In this situation there is no increased risk to the stockholders, since they own the debt, but the form of the distribution of earnings is changed.

With all the capital in the form of stock, the cash distributions to the owners would not result in a tax deduction. With all the capital in the form of debt, an amount equal to the tax rate times the cash distribution would be a tax saving. To avoid being identified as a "thin corporation" the firm would want less than 100% debt, and to avoid arousing the Internal Revenue Service it would not want to issue all its debt to the stockholders. But assuming the firm did not go too far, it is clear that in the presence of current income tax laws one can change the value of a corporation's earning stream by changing its capital structure. The clearest illustration of benefit arises when we merely change the form of the distribution (a dividend changed to interest) but where the payments are made to the same capital contributors. Where the payment is made to a third party who is not presently a stockholder, the analysis becomes more complex because the risk changes.

A corporation that has debt outstanding, or is issuing debt, is better off with interest being deductible than not deductible, for tax purposes. For example, assume that interest is deductible and that debt is outstanding with an interest rate of 0.05 and the marginal tax rate is 0.4 (the after-tax interest rate is 0.03). We further assume that the time value of money of both stockholders and bondholders is 0.05. In this situation, the deductibility of interest for tax purposes enables the firm to undertake investments for the benefit of the stockholders with yields of less than 0.05 (but with after-tax yields of at least 0.03). Without the deductibility of interest, investments yielding less than 0.05 would be rejected.[5] The investments are desirable with yields between 0.03 and 0.05 because of a combination of tax deductibility of interest and trading on the equity.

With investments yielding over 0.05, financed by the 0.05 debt, the stockholders again benefit, but with investments yielding over 0.05, we have a situation of pure trading on the equity, and the acceptability of the investment is not the result of the tax deductibility of interest (although the fact that interest is deductible may make the investment more desirable.)

EXAMPLE

Assume that $1000 of debt paying $50 of interest is issued. The amount available for stockholders is illustrated assuming different after-tax earnings.

		Situation			
		1		2	3
After-tax returns		$30		$50	$ 80
Interest:	$50		$50		$50
Less:					
tax saving	20	30	20	30	20	30
Net gain to stockholders		$ 0		$20	$ 50
Total amount distributed					
to capital contributors		$50		$70	$100

There is no gain to stockholders when the investment returns only the after-tax yield of the bond. In the second situation, there is a net gain to the stockholders of $20 that would not exist if the interest were not deductible for tax purposes. In the third situation, the stockholders are $50 better off; $30 is a result of trading on the equity, and $20 is a result of the tax saving.

[5] Insurance (risk-reducing) type investments are not considered here.

If the entire investment had been financed by common stock funds, the amounts available for distribution in the three situations would be $30, $50, and $80 instead of the $50, $70, and $100 distributed to the capital contributors when the $1000 of debt is used.

The Change in the Value of the Firm

The model that follows makes very special assumptions, and other assumptions would lead to modified results. We assume that it is correct to use the cost of debt as the discount factor for time, and that all the cash flows resulting from the operations of the firm should be discounted at the same rate of interest in computing the value of the firm.

Let us assume that an investor can discount for time using k. With a tax rate of t_c, the present value of constant before tax earnings X is:

$$V_0 = \frac{X(1-t_c)}{k}.$$

If we add an amount of debt B that pays k interest, and if we assume that all time discounting should be done using k, we obtain for the value of the levered firm.

$$V_L = V_0 + Bt_c$$

The first term on the right-hand side is the value with zero debt, and the second term is the value change resulting from issuing B of debt in substitution for common stock. If X is uncertain, it would be reasonable to also have a "risk adjustment" term subtracted to compute the value of the firm after the debt addition.

With a different assumption about how risk and time value should be taken into consideration, we can obtain different measures of the effect of adding debt. However, this is illustrative of the general approach.

It is interesting that with zero debt the amount available for capital contributors is $X(1 - t_c)$ each year, and with debt the cash flow is increased to $X(1 - t_c) + kBt_c$. This amount is independent of risk attitudes and discount rates.[6]

---

[6]This is partial analysis, since to be complete we should also consider personal income taxes.

Tax Considerations and Costs of Different Capital Sources

Assume for illustrative purposes that holders of bonds, preferred stock, and common stock of the ABC Company all required a return of 0.10, and there is a 0.4 tax rate. There are $1000 of each security outstanding (the return to each type of security is $100).

In order to have $100 to distribute to each type of security, the company will have to earn $434 before tax.

Table 9.2

	Before Interest, Before-tax Earnings	(1-tax Rate)	Necessary After-tax Earnings
Bonds	100		100
Preferred stock	167	0.6	100
Common stock	167	0.6	100
	434		300

Since the bond interest is deductible for tax purposes, we need only $100 of before-tax earnings to satisfy the interest payment to the bondholders.

If we take the ratio of the necessary after-tax earnings to the capital contributed, we find that the cost of each type of security is 0.10 (we could also say that the return to each type of investor is 0.10).

But let us consider more exactly the after-tax cost of debt. The $100 of interest results in a tax saving of $40, thus the net cost of the debt is $60 or 0.06 (60/1000 = 0.06). We can extend Table 9.2 to show the after-tax cost of each security (Table 9.3).

Table 9.3

	Necessary After-Tax Earnings[a]	Tax Saving[b]	Net Cost to Corporation
Bonds	100	40	60 or .06
Preferred stock	100	0	100 or .10
Common stock	100	0	100 or .10

[a]From Table 9.2
[b]Equal to the tax rate times the tax-deductible interest.

We have three sets of costs. These are set forth in Table 9.4.

Table 9.4. Costs of Each Type of Capital

	Necessary Earnings Before Tax[a]	After-Tax Distribution As a Fraction of Capital[a]	After-Tax Cost[b]
Bonds	0.10	0.10	0.06
Preferred stock	0.17	0.10	0.10
Common stock	0.17	0.10	0.10

[a]From Table 9.2.
[b]From Table 9.3. Each number in this column is 0.6 of the same line of column 1 of this table.

Instead of assuming that the returns of each type of security are equal, we now assume that the returns are 0.10 for debt, 0.12 for preferred stock, and 0.20 for common stock. The magnitude of these costs is consistent with experience. Table 9.5 shows the costs of the alternative sources:

Table 9.5. Costs of Each Type of Capital

	Before-Tax Necessary Earnings	After-Tax Distribution	After-Tax Cost
Bonds	0.100	0.10	0.06
Preferred stock	0.200	0.12	0.12
Common stock	0.334	0.20	0.20

In the current example, the common stockholders require twice as large a return as the bondholders, but the before-tax cost is more than three times as large. The difference in cost between preferred stock and bonds is also interesting. The preferred stock is twice as expensive as the bonds, despite the fact that the return to the preferred stockholders is only 0.12 compared to 0.10 for bondholders.

The differences in the cost would be less dramatic if a tax rate less than 0.4 were used. A higher tax rate would make the cost differences more dramatic.

PERSONAL TAXES AND THE OPTIMAL CAPITAL STRUCTURE

The study of the optimal capital structure question has proceeded in three stages. First there was the no-tax situation offered by Miller and Modigliani in which a firm's cost of capital is not affected by the amount of debt. Second, the corporate income tax was introduced with the conclusion that a firm should issue as much debt as the Internal Revenue Service will allow. This section argues that it is necessary to advance to the third stage, the introduction of personal income tax considerations. If we agree that business decisions cannot be made on a before-tax basis, the logical conclusion is that the investors' tax position as well as that of the corporation must be taken into consideration.

It is well known that the fact that a corporation can deduct interest in computing its taxable income acts as a significant incentive for corporations to issue debt. In fact it can be shown (without personal taxes) that firms should be financed by as much debt as the Internal Revenue Service will allow. This position has been stated frequently in the finance literature. It is argued here that the optimal capital structure of a corporation cannot be determined without consideration of the personal income taxes of the investors in the corporation.

There are three tax factors at work that must be considered in making capital structure decisions. First, there is the different treatment awarded interest and earnings of stockholders. Second, there is the possibility of a firm acting to defer the personal taxation of its stockholders by retaining rather than paying dividends and issuing new stock. Third, there is the differential tax rate applied to capital gains compared to that applied to ordinary income. The deductibility of interest moves a firm toward the use of debt, but the other two factors are strong incentives for issuing stock. The advantages of retention of earnings compared to cash dividends and issuing new stock to the present stockholders are well known. If interest payments are recognized to be the economic equivalent of dividends (although taxed differently), it can be seen that the twin advantages of tax deferral and capital gains with common stock may balance the disadvantage of losing the deductibility of interest.

The implication here is that the personal tax structure and tax situation of a corporation's investors should affect the capital structure of a corporation. The tax deferral and capital gains associated with common stock may outweigh the tax shield of debt interest.

WACC and Investments and Taxes

We want to show that if the return required by debt and stock can be defined for a given investment and a given capital structure, that the use of WACC as the required return will lead to the investors receiving their required returns. The analysis will include taxes.

Assume a corporation uses 1/3 debt and 2/3 stock to finance an investment. The stock has a cost of 0.15 and the debt costs 0.10 before tax. The tax rate is 0.4.

The WACC is

$$\text{WACC} = (1-0.4)(0.10)1/3 + (0.15)2/3 = 0.02 + 0.10 = 0.12.$$

Since the WACC is 0.12, an investment earning exactly 0.12 should just satisfy the investors. Assume an investment costing $300 is financed with $100 debt costing 0.10 and $200 stock equity costing 0.15 (this is consistent with the WACC of 0.12). The investment has a life of one year. To earn 0.12 an investment of $300 should earn $36 of income. The projected income statement for the project, exclusive of financing considerations is

Sales		$800
Cost of goods	$440	
Depreciation	300	
Tax	24	764
Income		$ 36

The after-tax cost of debt is 0.06, or for $100 it is $6, and the after-tax return to stock equity on their $200 investment is $30. The $36 of project income satisfies these earning requirements.

The funds flow is 36 + 300 = $336. This allows the payment of $6 after tax interest and $100 of principal to debt, $230 to stock, in the form of a $30 dividend and $200 return of capital.

The income statement, including the $10 interest expense, is

Sales		$800
Cost of goods	$440	
Depreciation	300	
Interest	10	
Tax	20	770
Income to Stockholders		$30

The funds flow to stock equity and principal payment (interest effects have already been considered) is $30 + 300 = $330, which is enough to return the $230 to stock equity investors and to pay the $100 principal of the debt.

To illustrate the effect of taxes on the cost of debt and the evaluation of an investment, now assume a one-period investment of $1000 and before tax flows of $1100 at time 1. The debt cost is 0.10.

The investment is marginally desirable, since the $1100 of investment cash flows will pay the investors the return they require.

Capital budgeting decision rules require that both the cash flows and the discount rate be on an after-tax basis. The cash flows for the investment are $-$1000 at time zero and $1060 at time 1.

Time 0	Time 1	
-1000	$+1100$	
	-40	Tax
	1060	Cash Flow After Tax

The after-tax discount rate is $0.10(1-0.4) = 0.06$, thus the investment is marginally acceptable.

It would have been an error to have used $1100 of cash flows at time 1 based on the logic that the firm actually pays zero tax (the $100 of income is tax shielded by the $100 of interest).

The conclusion is that the cash flows of the investment must be after tax *without* taking into consideration the tax shield provided by the method of financing. If returns to investors provide a tax shield, this is incorporated into the analysis by the computation of the after-tax discount rate.

CONCLUSIONS

This chapter has argued that the capital structure decision of a corporation depends on the personal tax rates of the investors in the corporation. Whether debt is more desirable than stock depends on the corporate tax rate, the personal ordinary income tax rate, and personal capital gains tax rate as well as the length of time that personal taxes will be deferred.

It is possible to avoid risk considerations by having the stockholders buy a mixture of stock and debt. If this procedure is objectionable, the capital structure decision becomes interwoven with the entire question of capital asset evaluation, since the expectation and the variance of the investor's returns will vary with the proportion of debt.

With the investors in a low tax bracket, there is a tendency for debt to be more desirable than stock, and this preference switches if the investors are from a high tax bracket. These conclusions assume that all the investment funds are to come from the present investors so that risk considerations do not enter the analysis.

Corporations generally have stockholders with tax rates ranging from zero (foundations, Universities, and retirees) to the maximum of the federal plus state and city taxes. In such a situation, the analysis of the chapter cannot be applied directly. It provides a reminder that different parties may desire the corporation to take different actions. The more information an investor has relative to corporate plans, the more likely the investor will be able to make decisions that are consistent with maximizing his own well-being.

We conclude that the cost to a firm of obtaining capital is a function of its capital structure. Thus with real-world institutions, the "cost of capital" is a variable dependent on the decisions of corporate managers.

CHAPTER 10

DIVIDEND POLICY

To pay or not to pay, that's the question.
Dividends give management indigestion.
Dividend checks make stockholders cheer,
But the company's growth will be small this year.
To maximize the stock price is what is sought.
It's a balancing act and takes much thought.

When General Motors Corporation designs an automobile, it designs a car for a specific segment of the market. When General Motors arrives at a dividend policy, it implicitly attempts to please all those who invest in common stock.

Walk into a financial vice-president's office of a major firm and announce that you have just advised a potential buyer not to buy the company's common stock. After the announcement, duck. Rather than the vice-president asking about the economic characteristics of the investor and why the purchase would not be reasonable, the reaction will be one of indignation. However, it is entirely appropriate that all corporations not appeal to all investors and that they design their common stock (and other securities) in the same way they design their consumer products. A corporation should have a financial personality resulting from its various financial policies (especially dividend policy) that is attractive to a given group of investors, and is inappropriate for other groups.

There have been two "golden rules" in respect to dividend policy followed by publicly held corporations. First, it is necessary to pay cash dividends to common stockholders, and second, the dividends through time must increase. It is far from obvious that these policies are optimum from the point of view of maximizing the well-being of all stockholders. In this chapter, we consider the effect of different dividend policies on the well-being of the common stockholders.

Before launching into examples that imply "exact" answers to the dividend versus no dividend decision, we describe several valid reasons for dividends. Some of these reasons cannot be quantified; thus they must be kept in mind in evaluating the decisions that result from the mathematical models.

REASONS FOR DIVIDENDS

One of the best reasons for a corporation to pay a dividend is that the corporation does not have good enough earning opportunities internal to the firm. Actually, formal dividend models handle this situation well, since the reinvestment earning rate of the firm is built into the models. Also the federal government supplies incentives in this situation. There is a provision in the Internal Revenue Code that penalizes the retention of earnings just to avoid income taxes. Although it is infrequently applied, this provision does exist as a threat to a corporation that retains and invests in "strange" ways. No corporation would want to pay the tax penalties associated with an excessive retention of earnings.

The attitude of investors is an important factor to be considered. Consistently increasing dividends are generally welcomed by investors as indicators of profitability and safety. Uncertainty is increased by lack of dividends or dividends that fluctuate widely. Also, dividends are thought to have an information context; that is, an increase in dividends means that the board of directors expects the firm to do well in the future.

Since trust officers can only invest in securities with a consistent dividend history, firms like to establish a history of dividends so that they can make the "trust legal list." This consideration sometimes leads to the payment of cash dividends before the firm would otherwise start paying. Another important reason for the payment of dividends is that a wide range of investors needs the dividends for consumption purposes. Although such investors could sell a portion of their holdings, this latter transaction has relatively high transaction costs compared to cashing a dividend check. The presence of investors desiring cash for consumption makes it difficult to change the current dividend policy, even where such a change is dictated by the logic of the situation. Although one group of investors may benefit from a change in dividend policy, another group may be harmed. Although we see that income taxes tend to make a retention policy more desirable than cash dividends, the presence in the real world of zero tax and low tax investors dictates that we consider each situation individually and be flexible in arriving at a dividend policy.

One clever device that has been used to allow for relatively rapid growth in dividends while conserving some cash is for the majority stockholder to forego dividends for a period of time. For example, if the earnings are $10 million, there are 10 million shares outstanding, and the company is paying $1 per share cash dividend, it would appear that all the earnings are being paid out. However, if the majority stockholder, owning 50% of the shares, foregoes a cash dividend, the $1 per share dividend uses only $5 million of the earnings. Although this does facilitate higher dividends than could otherwise be paid (while the firm still retains earnings), it also results in a loss of earning opportunities to the majority stockholder. It is possible that this strategy might result in a higher price for the stock than would otherwise occur, but it is also possible that the most important result is a loss of current dividends to the majority stockholder.

We next consider a series of examples of retention versus dividends. It should be kept in mind that the conclusions resulting from the examples should be tempered with the types of reasons that are described in this section.

RETENTION VERSUS DIVIDEND: TAX DEFERRAL

It has been "proven" that dividend policy is not relevant to the valuation of the common stock equity of a firm. However, the proof assumes zero personal taxes; thus it does not apply to a real-world situation in which such taxes exist.

In the real world, an investor benefits from being able to defer the payment of taxes as well as the fact that some types of income (capital gains) are taxed at lower rates than other types of income.

If a company retains $100, earns 0.10 per one period, and then pays a dividend of $100, the investor taxed at a rate of 0.6 will net:

$$\$110 \ (1 - 0.6) = \$44.$$

If the same company had paid a dividend of $100 and if the investor also could earn 0.10 before tax and 0.04 after tax on the $40 reinvested funds, the investor receiving the dividend would have after one period:

$$40 \ (1.04) = \$41.60.$$

The investor is better off by $2.40 with the one-period delay in cash distribution. The investor "defers" $60 of taxes that earns 0.04 or $2.40; thus the investor is better off by $2.40.

If desired, one could compute the return necessary for the firm to earn to justify retention. It would be equal to the after-tax return (0.04) available to the investor. Thus if the corporation could earn 0.04 and then pay a dividend, the investor would net:

$$\$100 \ (1.04) \ (1 - 0.6) = \$41.60.$$

This is the same as he would net with an immediate cash dividend.

If the planning horizon is n periods instead of one, then 0.04 still measures the return that the firm must earn to justify retention. If the earning opportunities are greater than 0.04, retention is more desirable than an immediate dividend.

If the planning horizon is n periods, the dollar advantage of tax deferral increases. For example, if the time horizon is 20 years with retention the investor has:

$$100 \ (1.10)^{20} \ (1 - 0.6) = 100 \ (6.73) \ (0.4) = \$269.$$

if the firm can earn 0.10.

With an immediate cash dividend and the investment of $40 by the stockholder to earn 0.04 after tax for 20 years, the investor would have:

$$40 \ (1.04)^{20} = 40 \ (2.191) = \$88.$$

The difference in favor of retention is $181. If we had assumed that the reinvestment from the dividends was not taxed currently, we would have obtained a slightly smaller benefit for retention, but of the same magnitude.

With a planning horizon of 20 years, the advantage of tax deferral is $181 for the retention in the one year generating the earnings. There will be 19 other years between now and the end of the 20 years that will generate comparable tax deferral savings (although of decreasing amounts). If we find the value at the end of 20 years of all the tax deferral savings for the 20 years, we find the savings are $1102.[1]

CAPITAL GAINS

To this point we have assumed that all income is taxed at one rate. Now we assume that a capital gains tax rate of 0.3 applies to income that is deferred. This assumes that retention of earnings leads to stock price increases and that these increases can be realized by investors if they desire. For example, if the firm retains $100 and earns 0.10 after one period the firm will have $110. If this $110 is readily available for dividends, the stock value should be close to $110, since the prospective cash dividend is worth $110. If the investor prefers capital gains to cash dividends, the stock can be sold prior to the ex-dividend date and the gain taken in the form of a capital gain.

If we shift to the 20-year horizon, with retention and then capital gains taxation of 0.3, the investor would have:

$$100 \ (1.10)^{20} \ (1-0.3) = 100 \ (6.73) \ (0.7) = \$471.$$

The cash dividend and an after-tax earning rate of 0.04 again leads to a value of $88.

The net advantage of retention is $471 - 88 = $383.

Capital gains taxation increases the value of retention from the $181 obtained above to $383.

Again, if we considered the tax consequences of all the years, the value of the difference would be even larger.

[1]The savings are equal to $\displaystyle\sum_{n=1}^{20} 100(1.10)^n(0.4) \ -\sum_{n=1}^{20} 40(1.04)^n$

A CONSTANT INVESTMENT POLICY

The previous examples implicitly assumes that the amount of investment undertaken by the firm is affected by the dividend-retention decision.

We now assume that the investment policy of the firm has been established, and the investments that will take place in the next n years will not be affected by the dividend policy. Further, we assume that if a dividend is paid, the funds required to implement the investment policy will come from the present stockholders.

This type of policy, although it seems strange (to give money to investors and then request the funds back), is frequently found in the real world. The situation exists when a dividend-paying company concurrently raises funds either in the form of common stock, preferred stock, or debt from its present stockholders.

The advantage of zero dividends compared to a series of cash dividends is equal to the sum of present values of the taxes saved on *not* having the cash dividends *less* the present value of capital gains tax paid at the end of the time horizon, because the cash contributed by the investors (equal to the cash dividends) did not increase the investors tax basis. A numerical example follows.

EXAMPLE

Let the tax rate on ordinary income be 0.7 and on capital gains be 0.25. The investor can earn 0.03 after tax. The initial dividend is \$1, and dividends will grow at 0.10 per year.

We assume a five-year planning horizon.

We would have the following dividends and present values:

Year n	Dividend	$(1.03)^{-n}$	Present Value of Dividend
1	1.00	0.9709	0.9709
2	1.10	0.9426	1.0369
3	1.21	0.9151	1.1073
4	1.331	0.8885	1.1826
5	1.4641	0.8626	1.2629
Total dividends	6.1051		5.5606 Present value of dividends

The advantage of zero dividends compared to current dividends increasing through time is the present value of taxes saved:

$$0.7(5.5606) = \$3.89$$

less the present value of value of the tax basis lost since zero investment was made, times the tax rate:

$$0.25(6.1051)\,(1.03)^{-5} = \$1.32 \text{ or } \$3.89 - 1.32 = \$2.57.$$

The advantage of zero dividends for five years compared to the dividend policy of paying $1 and increasing the dividend by 10% per year, is $2.57 per dollar of present dividends.

If the time horizon had been for $n = 20$ instead of $n = 5$, the advantage of a zero dividend policy would have been $19.32 per dollar of current dividend. If the current dividend had been $10 per year instead of $1, the advantage for $n = 20$ would have been $193.25

Because the investment policy is assumed to be independent of the dividend-retention decision, the value of the firm after n periods is common to both decisions (dividends or retention).

This value drops out when we compute the net advantage of the zero dividend policy. Thus the advantage of retention is not dependent on a forecast of future value (remember the investment policy of the firm is assumed to be fixed).

Although the example seems far fetched (why would a company pay a dividend of $D dollars and have the investor invest the same amount back in the firm), many firms are embarking on so-called "dividend reinvestment" plans whereby dividend checks go directly to a bank where the funds are reinvested in the common stock of the same firm. The net results of plans such as this are very similar to the example of this section.

CONCLUSIONS

If an investor in a high tax bracket expects the price of a stock to increase because of improved earnings (and a higher level of future dividends), he will be willing to pay more for a stock knowing that if his expectations are realized the stock can be sold and be taxed at the relatively lower capital gains tax rate. Whereas the capital gains tax treatment tends to increase the value of a share of stock, we have shown that another powerful factor arises from the ability of the stockholder to defer paying taxes if the corporation retains income rather than paying dividends. Tax deferral is an extremely important advantage associated with the retention of earnings by a corporation.

It is not being argued that all firms should discontinue dividend payments. There is a place for a variety of payout policies, but there is a high cost to investors for all firms attempting to cater to the dividend and reinvestment preferences of an average investor. The firm that combines dividend payments with the issuance of securities to current investors is causing some of its investors to pay unnecessary taxes, as well as incurring increased transactions costs itself in raising the funds.

A board of directors acting in the interests of the stockholders of a corporation sets the dividend policy of a firm. The ability of an investor to defer income taxes as a result of the company retaining earnings is an important consideration. In addition, the distinction between ordinary income and capital gains for purposes of income taxation by the federal government accentuates the importance of the investor knowing the dividend policy of the firm whose stock he is considering purchasing or has already purchased. In turn, this means that the corporation (and its board) has a responsibility to announce its dividend policy, and attempt to be consistent in its policy, changing only when its economic situation changes significantly. In the particular situation in which a firm is expanding its investments rapidly and is financing this expansion by issuing securities to its stockholders, the payment of cash dividends is especially vulnerable to criticism.

The planning of investment decisions and dividend policy must be coordinated so that the well-being of the firm's stockholders is incorporated in the planning process. The corporate planners should realize that the individual investors are also making plans, and the corporation can assist this planning process by making its own plans well known.

Chapter 11

REACQUISITION OF COMMON STOCK BY THE CORPORATE ISSUER

When a company buys its own shares it's called
A stock acquisition.
Both good and bad results. We have
An ambivalent position.
Tax benefits surely are good, but the firm
Shrinks in size.
Regretably business does not come
Sanforized.

While companies acquired their own shares during the 1960s, in the early 1970s, the use of share repurchase exploded. By 1973 the corporate acquisition of a corporation's own shares was running at a rate of over $3 billion per year. Explanations offered by managers for the acquisition of shares are generally intuitively appealing, but few of them will stand up to careful scrutiny. We want to consider the *announced* reasons for acquisition and the *real* reasons why acquisition may well be desirable to the purchasers of common stock.

The reasons for share acquisition and the implications for the theory of share valuation and for public policy have been subject to numerous, and often conflicting, interpretations. This chapter presents an analysis of the economics of share repurchasing that leads to some fairly definite conclusions concerning the desirability of share acquisition.

Some of the ideas of this chapter are based on an article with the same title by Harold Bierman, Jr. and Richard West published in the December 1966 issue of *The Journal of Finance*, pp. 687–696.

THE BACKGROUND

It is not difficult to illustrate the dimensions to which corporate share repurchasing has recently grown. A survey of the repurchasing activities of companies listed on the New York Stock Exchange revealed that in 1963, for example, 132 firms "repurchased enough of their own common shares to account for 5% or more of the total trading in their securities."[1] Share purchasing was, in fact, such a popular corporate activity in 1963 that "the total dollars spent by companies to buy back their common shares was 30% greater than the amount which they raised through (new) equity issues."[2] Moreover, in both 1964 and 1965, manufacturing, commercial, and transportation corporations continued to be net purchasers of stock.[3]

The growth of corporate share repurchasing has aroused considerable interest, and a number of explanations of the motivation behind this activity have been suggested. It has been argued, for example, that firms sometimes buy back their own shares to have them available to acquire other companies or to fulfill the obligations of stock option plans.[4] Unquestionably, some repurchasing has been done for these reasons. Income tax considerations may make it possible for firms to acquire other companies more cheaply for stock than for cash, and the use of stock options as a form of executive compensation has been widespread. However, it seems quite unlikely that the rapid growth of share repurchasing in recent years can be explained by merger and stock option plans. If the market price of the common stock currently reflects its value (that is, the stock is not underpriced), the current stockholders should be indifferent between the firm using reacquired shares or newly issued shares.

---

[1]Leo Guthart, "More Companies are buying Back Their Stock," *Harvard Business Review* Vol. 43, No. 2 (March-April, 1965), p. 40.

[2]James Fleck, "Corporate Share Repurchasing: An Informal Discussion," *Harvard Business School Bulletin*, Vol. 41, No. 1 (Jan-Feb, 1965), p. 10.

[3]The net change for all corporations during these years, however, was positive due to the sales of new securities by public utilities and real estate and investment companies. For more detail on this point, see the *Federal Reserve Bulletin*, May, 1966, p. 716.

[4]Eugene Brigham, "The Profitability of a Firm's Repurchase of Its Own Common Stock," *California Management Review*, Vol. VII, No. 2 (Winter, 1964), p. 69 and Charles Ellis, "Repurchase Shares to Revitalize Equity, "*Harvard Business Review*, Vol. 43, No. 4 (July-Aug, 1965), p. 120.

EXAMPLE

The ABC Company currently has 1 million shares outstanding and is earning $1 million or $1 per share. The company has $1 million of extra cash. The stock is selling at $10 per share, reflecting a price earnings ratio of 9 plus $1 per share extra cash.

The company can purchase for $1 million of cash or 100,000 shares of stock a firm that earns $111,111 per year.

BUY BACK SHARES

If the firm buys back 100,000 shares at a cost of $1 million and then issues them in connection with the acquisition, the earnings per share will be

$$\text{EPS} = \frac{\$1,111,111}{1,000,000} = \$1.11$$

With a price earning ratio of 9, this is a price per share of $10 (there is zero excess cash).

ISSUE NEW SHARES

If 100,000 new shares are issued the EPS is

$$\text{EPS} = \frac{\$1,111,111}{1,100,000} = \$1.01$$

Multiplying by 9 gives 9.09, and adding $1,000,000/1,100,000 = 0.91$ per share for the $1 million extra cash again gives $10 per share.

USE CASH

If cash is used for the acquisition, the EPS again equals $1.11 and with a P/E of 9 this leads to a value per share of $10.

This example shows that there is no benefit for share acquisition if the stock is fairly priced initially (this conclusion can also be shown algebraically).

Thus with fairly priced stock there is no essential reason why shares used for mergers and acquisitions or for stock options should be repurchased, rather than newly issued. Also, the chronologies of merger and stock option activities have not paralleled the growth of share repurchasing with sufficient regularity to indicate a causal relationship between these developments. The postwar merger movement was in full swing long before corporations began buying back their own shares in significant amounts, and the decline in the attractiveness of stock option plans because of the changes in the tax code has not been accompanied by a reduction in the amount of repurchasing.

Corporations also repurchase shares with the intention of retiring them or at least holding them indefinitely in the treasury. Several motives for such repurchasing activities have been suggested, virtually all relating the repurchase of the shares to the generation of liquid assets that cannot be profitably invested by the firm in the foreseeable future. In particular, it has been suggested that firms with "redundant" liquid assets have one or more of the following motives to repurchase shares:

1. Repurchasing shares is the best investment that can be made with these assets.

2. Repurchasing shares has beneficial leverage effects that cannot be obtained by distributing these assets to stockholders in another form, such as dividends.

3. Repurchasing shares, rather than paying dividends, has significant tax advantages for stockholders.

In view of the fact that U.S. corporations have experienced an unprecedented growth in liquidity over roughly the same period that stock repurchasing has flourished, the explanations listed above merit consideration. Is a firm's purchase of its own common stock an investment? Does a firm repurchase stock to produce leverage effects not otherwise attainable? What are the tax advantages associated with buying back shares?

The next section is devoted to a discussion of the investment and leverage questions. In brief, we argue that repurchasing is *not* an investment and does not produce "special" leverage effects. We then consider the argument that repurchasing shares can have beneficial tax effects for stockholders.

SHARE REPURCHASING AS AN INVESTMENT AND AS A MEANS OF INFLUENCING CAPITAL STRUCTURE

In this section we examine the logic underlying the arguments that, when a firm is generating more cash than it can profitably invest internally, share repurchasing (1) is itself a good investment and (2) can have beneficial leverage effects.

The Investment Question

The argument that share repurchasing involves some sort of investment seems widely held. Share repurchasing does not possess the same general characteristics as other acts of investment, for example, purchasing plant and equipment. Normal investments keep the size of the firm intact or increase it and either have no effect on the stockholders' equity balance or the number of shares outstanding, or increase them. A firm's acquisition of its own common stock, on the other hand, reduces the size of the enterprise. In particular, the cash balance is decreased, the stockholders' equity balance is reduced, and the number of shares outstanding is cut back. In short, repurchasing shares has few characteristics that identify it as a normal investment.

However, even though share repurchasing is not an investment, it may be the best use of corporate cash from the point of view of the present investors. This may occur if the present stock price is below the intrinsic value of the shares.

Market prices are set by investors based on available information. It is possible that decision makers of a firm may have more information than the market. In such a situation, ethical issues arise dictating against the firm acquiring its own shares. It is highly likely that some purchases take place in order for one group of investors to take advantage of inside information. Lacking the resources to buy the stock themselves, they use the corporation as the vehicle for making their investment. Another reason for purchase is that one group of stockholders currently controlling the corporation may seek to retain control. Again, lacking the financial resources as individuals, they use the corporation's resources to attain their own objective. We consider both of these reasons for purchase to result in improper activities by a corporation. The possibility of these situations developing is a cost of allowing corporations to repurchase their own shares.

However, let us assume that the market has all the available information, so that it is not a matter of ethics, but the stock price is lower than management thinks it should be based on the available published information. In such a situation, if the firm announces that it intends to follow a policy of stock acquisition, this may be the best use for the cash it possesses. However, this conclusion implicitly requires the presence of either personal income taxes or transaction costs. Without taxes or transaction costs, there is no real advantage of stock acquisition compared to a straight cash dividend.

Repurchasing and Leverage

Let us assume a situation in which a firm has decided that more leverage was desirable. One solution is for firms to regain an "optimal capital structure" by buying back their own shares and retiring them.

If we accept the argument that there is an optimal capital structure, we are still faced with the question: why repurchase shares to change the debt/equity ratio, rather than pay dividends or issuing debt? Buying back stock involves no changes in capital structure that could not also be obtained by combining a dividend payment with a reverse stock split. Both procedures have the effect of distributing cash to stockholders, reducing the firm's capitalization and the number of outstanding shares, increasing its earnings per share, and thereby raising the stock price per share (compared to what it would have been if the number of shares had not been reduced). Repurchase of shares is a very awkward way of adjusting capital structure.

Summing up, our analysis thus far suggests that it is unlikely that the recent growth in share repurchasing can be accounted for on the grounds that it has been done (1) to provide shares to be used for mergers or stock options, (2) to "invest" redundant liquid assets, or (3) to produce changes in leverage.

TAXES AND SHARE REPURCHASING

The current tax laws provide powerful incentives for firms with redundant liquid assets to repurchase shares rather than pay dividends.

Tax Benefits to Shareholders

Under the present tax structure, many persons prefer capital gains to ordinary income. The reason for their preference is that the marginal rate of taxation on ordinary income can range as high as 70%, whereas the rate on long-term capital gains is only one-half that on ordinary income, up to a maximum rate that is far below that applied to ordinary dividend income.

Consider now a corporation with excess liquid assets that it desires to pay out in the form most attractive from its shareholders' point of view. If it distributes them as dividends, they will represent ordinary income to shareholders, and will be taxed accordingly. If, on the other hand, the corporation buys back shares, a portion of its distribution will be regarded as a return to the shareholders' capital and will not be taxed at all, whereas that portion of the return that is taxed, that is, the capital gain, will be subject to a lower rate than ordinary income. In addition, the investor who merely wants to reinvest is not taxed at all, since he does not sell his stock.

Given these incentives for returning cash to stockholders by repurchasing shares, a relevant question would seem to be: Why do firms ever pay dividends? We suspect that the answer is related to the attitude of the Internal Revenue Service toward share repurchasing. The current Internal Revenue Code clearly seeks to prohibit firms from disguising dividends in the form of share repurchases. Proportional repurchases, for example, are treated the same as dividends for tax purposes. Thus, if firms began to make all distributions in the form of share repurchase, they would almost certainly bring forth a response from the IRS.

But why then have firms begun to repurchase shares in increasing amounts? One possible rationalization is that they feel they can defend their recent activities on nontax grounds, for example, on the grounds that they are making investments or simply adjusting leverage. Second, the IRS has been permissive and has allowed a large amount of share repurchasing.

EXAMPLE

Assume a personal tax rate of 0.7 and a capital gains tax rate of 0.3. The investor's common stock has a tax base of $40.

If the investor receives $40 in the form of a cash dividend, he will net out $12 after paying $28 of tax.

If the investor receives $40 from the sale of one share of stock, he will net out $40.

One must be careful about real and illusory changes that take place with stock repurchasing. For example, in this illustration, a casual reader might be upset because with the cash dividend the investor retains all shares, whereas with stock acquisition the investor sells a share of his holdings. Let us expand the example. Assume that the investor owns 0.01 of the firm (say 100 shares out of 10,000) and that the corporation has enough cash to buy back 500 shares or 0.05 of the outstanding shares at $40 per share. This is $20,000. With a cash dividend, the investor will receive $2 per share of $200 in total and will own 0.01 of the firm. With a stock repurchase program, the investor could decide to sell 0.05 of his shares. He would then receive $200 of cash and would retain 95 shares.

The company would have 9500 shares outstanding; thus the investor would again own 0.01 of the shares outstanding. In both cases (with a cash dividend and with stock repurchase), the investor has $200 cash and 0.01 ownership in the firm. The only true difference is the tax treatment the investor will face under the two different corporate policies.

Repurchasing and Share Valuation

We have argued that tax considerations are an important explanation of corporate repurchasing of stock. It is desirable for us to attempt to specify how a firm's decision to repurchase stock rather than pay dividends might be expected to influence share prices.

We now consider how the choice of the form of a company's cash distribution (as between dividends and share repurchasing) influences stock valuation in a world in which ordinary personal income and capital gains are both taxed. Assume that all individuals are subject to a personal income tax rate of t_p and that the corporation distributes earnings of t_p D dollars per period as dividends. If the dividends are constant through time and if the stock at the beginning of the current period will be

$$V_0 = \frac{(1 - t_p) D}{k} .$$

Now assume that the firm announces it will distribute its earnings by repurchasing stock rather than paying dividends. Furthermore, let us assume (1) that present shareholders desire to keep their percentage ownership interest in the firm intact over time, and thus each period sell a proportion of their holdings equal to the proportion of the total shares retired, and (2) immediately following its share repurchasing, the firm declares a stock dividend large enough to replace the shares retired; that is, the number of shares outstanding at the beginning of any period n is constant.

Given these assumptions, and letting t_g be the tax rate on capital gains, we can now write[5]

$$V_0 = \frac{D}{2} \left[\left(1 + \frac{4(1 + k - t_g)}{k^2} \right)^{1/2} - 1 \right]. \tag{11.2}$$

An inspection of equation (11.2) reveals that in a world in which capital gains and ordinary income are accorded different tax treatment, the value of the firm's stock is influenced by the form of its cash distribution. It should be noted that the models presented could be adjusted to include fluctuating corporate earnings, various payout ratios, a progressive income tax, uncertainty, and so on. Naturally, such adjustments would significantly complicate the mathematical statement of the problem and alter somewhat the relative attractiveness of share repurchasing and dividend payments. There are two factors at work, however, that cause buying back shares to be more profitable than dividend payments (from the stockholders' point of view) under any reasonable set of assumptions that includes taxation of income. For one thing, part of the distribution under the share repurchasing arrangement is considered a return of capital and is not taxed at all. Second, that part of the distribution subject to tax (i.e., the capital gain) is generally taxed at a lower rate than ordinary income.

EXAMPLE

Let $t_p = 0.7$, $t_g = 0.25$, and $k = 0.04$.

Assume constant dividends (cash distributions) of $1 million per year, the first distribution being due one period from now.

Assuming cash dividends:

---

[5]Derivation of the equation can be found in the journal article by Bierman and West, *op. cit.* Different assumptions will lead to slightly different forms of equation (11.2), but the results will not differ materially.

$$V_0 = \frac{(1 - 0.7)}{0.04}(1,000,000) = \$7,500,000.$$

If shares are reacquired, instead of a cash dividend:

$$V_0 = \frac{1,000,000}{2}\left[\left(1 + \frac{4(1.04 - 0.25)}{0.04^2}\right)^{1/2} - 1\right]$$

$$= 500,000\ [(2226)^{1/2} - 1] = 500,000 \times 46.2$$
$$= \$23,000,000.$$

Assume that there are 1 million shares now outstanding. Using stock acquisition instead of a cash dividend, the value of the stock to the investor increases from $7.50 per share to $23 per share. The immediate stock price may or may not go up, but the value to the holder of the stock does go up.

STOCK ACQUISITIONS: A FLEXIBLE DIVIDEND

One real advantage of stock acquisitions in lieu of cash dividends is that an investor who does not want to convert his investment into cash does not sell his stock back to the corporation. By not selling, he avoids realization of the capital gain and does not have any taxation on the increment to the value of his wealth (he also avoids transaction costs).

The investor who wants to receive cash sells a portion of his holdings, and even though he pays tax on his gain, it is apt to be less than if the cash distribution were taxed as ordinary income. By using stock acquisition as the means of the cash distribution, the company tends to direct the cash to those investors who want the cash and bypass the investors who do not need cash at the present time.

STOCK ACQUISITIONS: STOCK OPTION PLANS

A sometimes neglected consequence of stock repurchase programs is that such programs enhance the value of stock options compared to cash dividends by forcing the stock price up compared to a cash dividend (the number of shares outstanding is reduced). The increase in stock price is not a real advantage to the investor, but it is an advantage to the holders of stock options.

EXAMPLE

A firm has 1 million shares outstanding selling at $40 per share. If it pays a $4 million cash dividend, the value of the firm will be $36 million

CASH DIVIDEND

Stock price per share	$36
Cash received	4
Total value to investor per share	$40

STOCK REPURCHASE

The firm will buy 100,000 shares. The value of the firm after purchase will be $36 million, and the stock price per share will be $40 (that is, 36,000,000/ 900,000= $40). The investor is indifferent, but the holder of a stock option prefers the $40 market price to the $36 price with cash dividends.

CONCLUSIONS

Three public policy questions concerning corporate share repurchasing become apparent. First, should firms be allowed to buy back their own shares, and, if so, should they be required to give stockholders advance notice of their intentions for the future? Third, how should such distributions be taxed?

We have shown that repurchasing shares can have a significant impact on the after-tax returns of stockholders. Should the form of the firm's distribution, rather than its substance, influence the amount of taxes paid by stockholders? It seems clear that, as more and more firms become aware of the advantages of repurchasing shares compared with paying dividends, this issue will have to be faced.

Should corporations that decide to repurchase shares be required to notify stockholders of their intentions? We have shown that the value of the firm's stock is a function of the form of its cash distributions. Thus it seems reasonable that shareholders be advised of a company's distribution policy, and of changes in that policy. The corporation that repurchases shares without giving its stockholders advance notice is implicitly, if not explicitly, penalizing those who sell their shares without this information.

Here is another situation (as with capital structure and dividend policy) in which corporate financial planning affects the plans of individual investors. It is reasonable for individual investors to be informed of the financial plans of the corporation, where disclosure of the plans will not significantly adversely affect the competitive position of the firm.

CHAPTER 12

VALUATION OF A PROSPECTIVE ACQUISITION

Book value is irrelevant.
It merely tells you what you spent.
The present worth you must assay,
The sum of future flows today.

In a narrow sense, the problem of valuation of a firm arises when a firm is being considered for acquisition. In a broader sense, the problem arises whenever common stock of a corporation is being considered as an investment. We investigate only the former question, although the procedures have broader application. In each case we compute the present value of the stockholders' equity.

The value of the stockholders' equity may be computed using:

1. Book value
2. Liquidation value of the assets
3. Replacement costs
4. Market value of the stockholders' equity
5. The expected earnings times a price-earnings multiplier
6. Going concern value of the stockholders' equity (present value of the cash flows)

In practice we would expect the valuation to be accomplished using a combination of the above measures, with the actual offer being as much a matter of game theory as basic valuation. That is, having determined the value of the firm to be acquired, it is then necessary to determine the minimum amount that can be offered and still have a reasonable probability of acquiring the firm and making an income.

BOOK VALUE

Taking the book value of the assets and then subtracting the total liabilities to obtain the book stock equity is a point of departure for the valuation of an acquisition. Perhaps the most important consideration is that some of the present holders of the shares of the firm being acquired will consider the book value to be important (just as they might consider important the price that they paid, even though this too is a sunk cost, and thus it is not "relevant"). Thus in some situations the book value may be thought to be floor for an offer, not for economic reasons, but because of the likely thinking of sellers.

With knowledgable sellers and buyers, the book values of the assets become important only to the extent that they become the basis for recording the assets on the books of the acquiring firm (as they would with pooling of interests accounting). Aside from this, book value is not relevant to the economic analysis of the purchase (the book tax basis would be relevant). The accountant records sunk costs, and sunk costs are not relevant in evaluating an acquisition from an economic standpoint.

Although we would expect a firm with a book value of $5 billion to have more valuable real assets than a second firm with a book value one-tenth that size, this type of conclusion is better based on one of the other methods of valuation.

LIQUIDATION VALUE

The liquidation value of the assets of a firm sets a floor for the value of the firm. If the owners of the firm can obtain $x by liquidating, there is little economic reason for them to sell the firm for less than $x.[1] In like manner, the bidders may feel safe bidding the liquidation value because they believe that, if they cannot operate the enterprise successfully, they can liquidate.

The liquidation value may be defined as equal to the immediate sale value of the assets less the liabilities present (or that have to be assumed by the new plant owner). The liquidation value of assets, such as

[1]There may be noneconomic reasons for the owners to sell at less than liquidation value to keep the enterprise functioning, for example, loyalty to the community, pride in the enterprise, and so on.

inventory and plants, may differ widely from the accounting measures, and there is no justification for assuming that the accounting measures of value have any use in this context. Hopefully, the accounting records will contain information relative to physical quantities and location that will be useful in searching out the value of the assets.

With the possible exception of patents, it is likely that the intangible assets will have little value on liquidation. Occasionally, the name of the firm or product may be sold, but where the firm is being liquidated, it would not be surprising to find that goodwill has reached a value close to zero.

To compute the value of the stockholders' equity, the present value of the liabilities (which may be different than the book value) are subtracted from the liquidation value of the assets.

REPLACEMENT COST

In some situations, the acquiring firm is only interested in the production capacity of the prospective acquisition. That is, it is not buying the goodwill, the managerial team, the customers, and so on, but only the production capacity. In this type of situation, the replacement cost of facilities is highly relevant information, since the facilities could be built rather than acquired. Timing is frequently offered as the reason for the acquisition of a firm rather than starting from scratch. An acquisition is a quick way of obtaining production capacity or position in an industry.

MARKET VALUE OF THE STOCKHOLDERS' EQUITY

If there is a market value for the firm's stock, an attempt might be made to compute the value of the stockholders' equity based on the market valuation. One assumption that can be made is that we can multiply the number of shares outstanding by the current market price of the stock. This assumes that those people currently not selling their stock at the market price value their holdings at the market price. It can be argued that, with a closely held corporation, if the stockholders desire to unload their stock, they may not be able to, because the market is too thin. On the other hand, all investors holding or buying the stock are implicitly placing a higher than market value on the stock.

Can one obtain the value of the stockholders' equity by extending the market value for a few shares traded on the stock market? If more shares were offered for sale, it would not be surprising to see the price per share be somewhat lower than it is for normal daily trading. However, it should be remembered that the entire universe of investors is available as possible purchasers of the stock. It will not take a large price decline to attract the investors necessary to digest the additional shares of stock assuming the price before the shares were offered was set by the same market.

Most important, an acquiring firm will generally expect to pay more than the market value for shares of stock. The market value sets a floor for the bid price rather than being a feasible method of valuation for purposes of acquisition.

PRICE EARNINGS MULTIPLIER

The use of the expected earnings times a price earnings multiplier is a common technique for evaluating prospective acquisitions. If there is some type of synergy (2 + 2 = 5) associated with the acquisition, the acquiring firm's estimate of earnings will be higher than the market's estimate, and the firm can offer an attractive price to the present owners.

At its best, the use of a price earnings multiplier is a short-cut method of applying discounted cash flows. The following mathematical model illustrates this position.

Let

P be the market price per share
k be the discount rate
g be the growth rate in earnings and dividends
E be the earnings
b be the retention percentage

In Chapter 7 we showed that

$$P/E = \frac{(1-b)}{k-g}$$

Thus the price earnings ratio *(P/E)* is equal to the dividend payout rate $(1 - b)$ divided by $k-g$. The larger the value of the growth rate (g), the larger the value of the *P/E* ratio that will be justified, and if the market accepts the model, the higher the price earnings multiplier that will be observed.

Using the P/E Multiplier

If one were to determine a price earnings multiplier for a specific firm, in order to use the *P/E* ratio there remains the problem of determining the earnings to which this multiplier should be applied. Conceptually, it is easy to arrive at the fact that only future earnings are relevant. But the forecast of future earnings is apt to draw on the measurement of recent past earnings. Let us consider the 1975 earnings of the U.S. Steel Corporation to illustrate the difficulty of arriving at a single earnings number that we are enthusiastic about using for decision making.

For the year 1975, U.S. Steel reported net income of $560 million. Sales had decreased by $1 billion from 1974 (a 10% decrease), but return per dollar of sales remained a constant 6.7%, and return on stock equity only decreased from 14.2 to 11.5%. Income only decreased from $630 million in 1974 to $560 million in 1975.

Given the $1 billion decrease in sales, the ability to maintain the same profit per dollar of sales is both admirable and surprising. Let us consider the earnings of $560 million in somewhat more detail.

The following information was obtained from the U.S. Steel annual report. Income was increased by:

$45 million sale of "surplus" timberland

$34 million "LIFO Pool" reduction

$89 million of depreciation reduction despite an increase in depreciable assets arising from:

$35 of newly fully depreciated assets

$23 sale of Orinoco property to the Venezuelan Government

$31 variable depreciation reduction

$5 million currency devaluation (previously deferred)

$30 million change in pension accounting. The past service liability of 1.2 billion was previously written off over 15 years; now it is written off over 25 years

$51 million arising from the investment tax credit and the use of flow
   through

$20 million interest reduction despite an increase in debt

$11 million arising from sale of assets

$17 million arising from repurchase of own bonds

$5 million arising from change in accounting for labor costs

These numbers add up to $307 million. Subtracting $307 from $560 of
reported income gives a "hard income" measure of $253 million which
can be interpreted as a reasonable forecast for the next period's future
earnings if the same level of operations is attained and nothing else
changes. We do not intend to imply that there was something wrong
with the income being increased by the $307 million of items listed.
However, each of the items listed is worthy of thought and discussion.
The overall result is a reaffirmation of the fact that the reported
income of a firm cannot be accepted automatically as the number to be
used for decision making or for analysis. It is interesting that the
published annual report supplied all the information necessary to make
the adjustments described. Even if one were to accept the $560 as the
one single "best" measure of income, it is obvious that alternative
measures are also worthy of consideration and use.

GOING CONCERN VALUE OF THE STOCKHOLDERS' EQUITY

Having computed the liquidation value and market value of the firm, it
is necessary to compute the going concern value of the net assets (the
term "net" means net of liabilities). The going concern value of the net
assets will be equal to the present value of the future cash flows
resulting from operations, although there may have to be adjustments.
We compute the going concern value of the assets, not by looking at the
assets, but by looking at the future cash generation (indirectly using
future incomes, since the cash flows are highly dependent on the
projection of income). Capital investments reduce the cash flow of the
period in which the cash disbursements are made.

Using this method, it is necessary to appraise the assets to determine
if they are adequate for carrying out the forecast operations. Are they
more than adequate? If there are excess facilities that may be sold, the
expected proceeds may be used to decrease the purchase cost (that is,

the amount we pay will be reduced effectively by the cash we obtain from selling off the assets), and increase the amount we are willing to pay for the firm. The excess asset may be cash. If the firm being acquired has more cash than is needed to finance future operations, the excess cash may be considered to reduce the purchase cost (the amount we would be willing to pay is increased). However, if the cash on hand is less than that needed to run efficiently the enterprise, the purchase cost of the firm must be increased by this amount (the amount we are willing to pay is decreased). Any plant assets that will have to be acquired would also affect the cash flow of the period in which they will have to be acquired. An excessively large amount of accounts receivable may also be looked on as reducing the purchase cost, because, once converted into cash, this fund may be taken from the firm. The prime component of the computation is the present value of the cash flow, although the stock of assets is relevant to the decision to the extent that the assets differ from what is considered to be normal value needed for operations.

What is the cash flow of a period? The easiest (although not exact) explanation is that the cash flow is equal to the expected changes in the bank account of the firm. There are several exceptions. For example, the expected dividends to be paid should not be deducted in computing the cash flows. If the firm, once acquired, will operate as a division or subsidiary corporation, there may be opportunity costs connected with the operation of the enterprise. For example, the central office may have to spend time worrying about its problems, and although there are no cash disbursements connected with this time, there is a cost that should be included in the cash flow. Also, the acquisition may affect the sales of other parts of the present corporation by gaining know-how, by decreasing competition, or by stimulating sales in some manner (a small-loan corporation may acquire a retail chain selling appliances to broaden its market for loans).

Except for items of this nature, the bank account analogy holds. The projected events for the future are accounted for on a naive cash basis. The accrual basis of accounting is not being used. This may seem to be inconsistent with the suggestions of the earlier sections of this book, but this is not true. The cash flow procedure is conceptually correct for the purposes at hand.

The use of the cash flow instead of the income seems to be inconsistent with accrual accounting. Where we are interested in the income of each time period, it is suggested that the accrual method is to be preferred. The making of the sale significantly changes the financial health of the firm and should be recorded as affecting the income of the time period in which the sale is made. For purposes of making an investment decision, it is suggested that the moment of the cash collection is the relevant consideration. We are interested in the present value of the cash flow for decision purposes, and the specific period in which the event occurs is not in itself important. We are not interested in determining the well-being of each period (although the cash flow and its timing are important for purposes of determining the present value).

For example, assume a situation in which a sale of $105 is made at the beginning of period 1 and the collection is to be made at the beginning of period 2. Assume a 0.05 rate of discount. Following good financial accounting conventions, the revenues recorded at the beginning of period 1 would be the present value of $105. The revenues of period 2 are zero. Using the cash-flow method, the cash flow of period 1 is zero, and period 2 would have a cash flow of $105 which, when discounted to the beginning of period 1, would have a value of $100 (using a 0.05 rate of discount).

There is only a difference in the labels. The present value of $105 should be used as the value of the receivable and the revenue. The accrual method properly records $100 as revenue at the beginning of period 1. The cash-flow method would show $105 at the beginning of period 2, but discounted back to the present, this becomes $100, and the two methods are equivalent.

Frequently, the projections of the future are based on the accounting measures of income of the past. The analyst must be careful to adjust to the cash-flow basis the accounting information presented on an accrual basis. One important item affected is the elimination of depreciation of plant assets and the write off of any other long-lived assets, such as patents. Also, the tax computations of the old firm may not be indicative of the taxes for the new firm.

The old depreciation charges are not relevant because the price being paid for the assets will determine the depreciation expenses of the future. Will there be any depreciation expenses deducted in the cash flow analysis? Indirectly, yes, but there will not be any depreciation shown on the cash-flow projections of the individual periods. The depreciation expense is implicit in the cash outlays. The same is true for write-offs of other long-lived assets, such as patents or goodwill.

It should be remembered that we are preparing an economic analysis for a decision. This involves projections of the future, and the result of the projection will be a cash flow for each year and a net present value of the investment. If the firm is acquired, accounting reports in the future will be prepared in accordance with accepted accounting principles, and these will differ from the cash projections used in the investment analysis because the accounting reports will probably be prepared on an accrual basis.

We have spoken of a discounting process. This requires that we use some rate of interest to accomplish the discounting. Some would recommend the use of the cost of capital (a weighted average cost of all capital sources), but this is an inadequate device. Studies of decision making under uncertainty indicate that the use of the cost of capital of the firm being acquired is not the best method of taking uncertainty into consideration. We use the rate of interest attached to minimum risk debt securities to accomplish the discounting for time value of money. The present value must then be adjusted for risk consideration.

EXAMPLE 1

Assume that the position statement of Company XYZ is as follows:

Cash-like assets	4000	Liabilities	3000
Plant assets	2000	Stock equity	4000
Intangibles	1000		
	7000		7000

The income statement for the past year was as follows:

Revenues (on the Cash Basis)	10,000
Less:	
Expenses (Including 400 of depreciation and 200 of amortization of intangibles)	8,400
Income	1,600
Dividends on Common Stock	1,600
Increase in Retained Earnings	0

The rate of interest to be used is 0.10. It is assumed that there will be no changes in future operations, that the assets presently owned (with normal replacement of $600 a year) are sufficient for those operations, and that dividends will be equal to income.[2]

What is the maximum amount a purchaser should be willing to pay, assuming that the present flows will continue infinitely into the future? Assume that taxes will be the same in the future as in the past. The cash flow of each year will be:

Revenues	10,000
Out-of-pocket expenses	7,800
	2,200
Investment	600
Cash flow	1,600

Note that the cash flow as computed is equal to both the income and total dividends. The equality with income holds because the replacement investment is equal to the sum of the expenses not requiring cash outlays.

The formula for the present value of a perpetuity is:

$$\text{Present value} = \frac{C}{k}$$

where C is the cash flow of each period and k is the rate of discount. In the example being considered, the present value would be:

$$\text{Present value} = \frac{1,600}{0.10} = \$16,000.$$

[2]In this example, the write-off of long-lived assets (depreciation and like expenses) is equal to the amount of investment necessary to maintain the future incomes at a level of $1600 and thus maintain future dividends at the same level. Assume that the expense following conventional accounting was computed to be some amount different from $600, but that $600 is the amount of investment necessary to maintain the future earnings and dividends at the current level. In this case, the income for decision purposes should be computed using the $600 of required outlays, not the conventional depreciation. Here the accounting information is being used to make future decisions, not to appraise the results of past decisions.

It may be argued that $16,000 is too much to pay for a firm that has a book value of $4000. From the point of view of a going concern, and with the information as given, the future cash flow has a present value of $16,000, and the present value of the stock equity is $16,000. However, if we introduced risk considerations into the analysis, the amount we would pay for the firm might fall to $4000 or less.

These computations make the very bold assumption that the cash flows would continue for perpetuity. A shorter time period, such as 50 years, would have given a present value of:

$$\text{Present value} = 1600 \times B(50,0.10) = 1600 \times 9.9148 = \$15,864.$$

The $15,864 valuation assumes that the firm is worthless after 50 years. Any expected net terminal value should be discounted back to the present and added to the $15,864 to find the present value of the stockholders' equity.

It may be argued that the cash flow will not continue on a level basis for perpetuity or for 50 years, but may fluctuate. If this is the case, we might want to include specific forecasts of the cash flow of the future years to the extent we are willing to make forecasts. It is also possible to forecast a decay of future cash flow arising from competition and changing economic conditions. We can then use the following formula for a situation in which the cash flows are expected to decay:

$$\text{Present value} = \frac{C_0}{k-g}$$

Where C_0 is the cash flow of the first period, and g is the rate of decay of cash flow per period, a negative growth rate. Assume the $1600 of the first year is expected to decrease at a rate of 0.06 per year. The computations then become:

$$\text{Present value} = \frac{1,600}{0.10-(-0.06)} = \$10,000$$

The $10,000 should be compared with the two previous present values.

In addition to the decaying situation, there may be a situation in which it is expected that the cash flow will grow. If the growth rate is less than the discount rate, say 0.02, the following formula may be used:

$$\text{Present value} = \frac{1600}{0.10 - 0.02} = \$20,000.$$

The last model assumes that the growth will continue for perpetuity. Assuming growth for perpetuity is an even more drastic assumption than if we assume constant cash flow or decreasing flows over that time period. Although it is useful for obtaining the upper limit of a bid, it should not be the sole basis for valuation. Growth generally does not continue forever.

Instead of assuming that the growth continues for perpetuity, we could make the computations for shorter time periods and incorporate a value of the stock equity at that terminal date. The arithmetic would become more complex, but the method of analysis remains the same. There is no restriction on the assumptions we may wish to make about what is likely to occur in the future relative to the type and duration of growth or decay. The only requirement is that all the future values be brought into the analysis and that they be discounted back to the present using an appropriate rate of discount.

In determining the value of the firm in the previous examples, several different present values were obtained, depending on the assumptions made about the nature of the growth. What is the maximum amount that should be offered for the firm by a prospective purchaser? Let us assume that it is expected that $1600 will be earned in perpetuity, giving a present value of $16,000. This value is an expectation; more exactly, it is the mean value of a distribution of the possible present values that may occur. The true present value of the firm is unknown, and it may be higher or lower than $16,000, but if forced to make one guess (or the average of many guesses), our guess would be $16,000. Remember that the rate of interest used in the discounting process was 0.10 and incorporated no conscious allowance for the risk of not realizing the expectations.

It is possible that the market may look at this situation and be willing to pay more than $16,000 because of uncertainty (in this case, the market is searching for the type of risk—that is, dispersion in possible outcomes represented by this firm and paying a premium for its risk. It is more likely that the market is discounting risk, and the market value of an expected constant stream of $1600 for perpetuity will be less than $16,000. Thus we would likely offer less than $16,000, the exact amount being determined by our opinion of the market discount for risk of the type of firm being considered as an investment.

For each of the previous computations, we used the first year's net cash flow of $1600. This amount was obtained by computing the net cash flow of the period. It is also equal to dividends on stock for the period and the income. The restrictive assumptions are now relaxed.

EXAMPLE 2

We now assume that investment-type outlays of $1000 a year are required to maintain the revenues of $10,000. The current depreciation and amortization is $600 for the items that will require $1000 a year outlays in the future. The annual out-of-pocket expenses are still projected to be $7800. The computation of the cash flow is:

Revenues	10,000
Out-of-pocket expenses	7,800
Gross cash flow	2,200
Investment (required)	1,000
Cash flow	1,200

Assuming that constant cash flows are projected for perpetuity and the rate of time discount is 0.10, the present value of the firm is now:

$$\text{Present value} = \frac{1200}{0.10} = \$12,000.$$

It should be noted that the conventional measure of income with the $600 deduction for the write-off of the fixed assets would not be a valid measure to project into the future, because we know that it will require $1000 a year to maintain the gross flow of $2200 and revenues of $10,000. The use of the $1000 deduction and the measure called *cash flow* is consistent with maintaining the gross cash flow of the firm and measuring the present value of the funds that will be available for dividends. The use of the $600 deduction gives a $1600 income measure, but this $1600 will not be available for dividends if we want to maintain constant revenues in the future.

If we interpret the term *investment* to include both long- and short-term investments, the cash flow of a period is also equal to the dividends of the period.

It should be noted that, if we compute the present value of the dividends, the dividends are a function of future sales, costs, and investments, and thus indirectly a function of future incomes. The projection of dividends should take into consideration all factors affecting dividends, including the necessary acquisition of assets or the sell-off of unnecessary assets.

THE VALUE OF THE FIRM WITH DEBT

In the previous examples, the value of the stockholders' equity was computed directly, and there was no interest-bearing debt. We use the same basic example to compute first the value of the firm and then the value of the stockholders' equity, where there is interest-bearing debt.

Assume that $2500 of the $3000 liabilities were interest-bearing and had an interest rate of 0.10 and that there is $250 of interest included in other expenses in the income statement. The cash flow of the firm before deducting interest is now $1850 (that is, equal to the $1600 previously computed plus $250 of interest). We call V the present value of the interest-bearing liabilities and stockholders' equity, using the interest rate as the rate of discount:

$$V = \frac{1850}{0.10} = \$18,500.$$

Assuming that the $1850 will continue to be a constant amount in the future, the value of V is $18,500. Subtracting the interest-bearing debt of $2500, we obtain $16,000, the same value of the stockholders' equity that we previously computed by discounting the cash flow of $1600.

Instead of computing the present value of the dividends plus interest, we could compute the present value of the cash flows less the interest payments (this is equivalent to the dividends to the stockholders). In this example, the present value of the $1600 of dividends is $16,000, which is the same amount we obtained discounting the $1850 and then subtracting the interest-bearing debt. This equality occurs because the interest on the debt is equal to the rate of interest being used to accomplish the discounting.

These two methods of computing the value of the stock equity may be called the "firm income" and the "stock income" methods. If the interest rate on the debt is used to accomplish the discounting, both methods give the same present value. Shifting from perpetuities would introduce computational problems, but the same concepts would apply.

CONCLUSIONS

Accounting information must be adjusted for purposes of determining the value of a firm. The liquidation value of the assets sets a minimum price and value, but any value in excess of this minimum must find its justification in the present value of the projected cash flow expected to be generated in the future. The going concern value of the assets, with the assets gaining their value from the cash flow, is the relevant factor. The prime advantage to be gained by using cash flow versus conventional income are that it is theoretically correct and it does not tie us to the results of accounting procedures that are not designed for this specific type of decision. If the decision maker wants to use the current income as the basis for making his investment decision, care should be taken since the computation may not be equivalent to the use of cash flows. However, even if he does not use the income measure directly, the decision maker will use it indirectly as the basis for his evaluation of future dividends.

This chapter bypassed a discussion of the risk considerations associated with the valuation of prospective acquisitions. Risk is discussed in Chapter 15.

CHAPTER 13

MERGERS AND ACQUISITIONS

All business has an urge
To merge,
Big business to ingest
The rest.
When firms combine they always strive
For two plus two to equal five,
But sometimes lacking synergy
Sadly two plus two makes three.

The 1960s was a period of wheeling and dealing among corporations. There were many reasons for the flurry of mergers and acquisitions:

1. Synergy (real and imaginary), the process whereby 2 plus 2 was supposed to equal 5, but sometimes equaled 3
2. Financial considerations
3. Bargain prices and funny money
4. Psychological reasons (empire building by managers)
5. The reduction of risk
6. The P/E factor
7. Accounting—pooling and purchase accounting

We consider each of the reasons and evaluate its validity.

SYNERGY

There are many reasons why two firms may be more valuable after a merger than as separate entities.

1. One firm may be badly managed and the other firm may have managerial talent.
2. One firm may have assets (e.g., plant or liquid assets) that can be effectively used by the other firm, or intangible assets such as production know-how.
3. Horizontal integration—increase markets (and possibly reduce competition).
4. Vertical integration—increase operating efficiencies by integration of production.
5. Joint utilization of service facilities, or organization and elimination of duplication.

The likelihood of synergy cannot be assumed to exist in all merger situations. The merger of the Pennsylvania and New York Central Railroads is a prime example of a case in which the opposite of synergy took place (the total sum was much less valuable than the sum of the parts). The expected increased efficiency of a merger may never be realized. Even though synergy cannot automatically be assumed, there are still many situations in which the two component firms joined together are able to achieve efficiencies that increase the total of the earnings to a higher level than would exist if the firms were not merged.

Mergers and acquisitions sometime supply the means of acquiring productive capacity that would otherwise take long periods of time to construct. The acquisition of the entire firm may be a cheaper and more rapid means of acquiring productive capacity than planning and building a plant.

FINANCIAL

The financial reasons for mergers and acquisitions are both real and imaginary (and it is not always easy to classify the reason). Consider the reason that new capital is easier to raise with a large corporation than with a small corporation. Although this position is generally accepted, it is not at all clear that a small, profitable, well-managed firm has more difficulty raising capital than a Penn Central, Rolls Royce, or a Lockheed. The present tax laws do tend to encourage acquisitions, since a firm that has accumulated cash may find it more desirable to spend the cash acquiring another firm than paying a cash dividend or investing the funds internally (see the chapter on dividend policy). The personal tax laws are a strong incentive for acquisitions.

Another tax consideration is the estate tax. An impending estate tax bill may force an owner of a firm to go public so that his estate is liquid (and a public corporation is easier to value).

A third tax reason is that, if a firm has a tax loss that it cannot use, a second firm currently paying taxes will find the tax loss carryforward to be an asset.

One must be careful in appraising the financial implications of a merger. LTV acquired a steel company expecting a large cash flow throw off, but the actual cash flow was much less because of the necessity to replace and expand the steel-making facilities to maintain the cash flow from operations.

The debt capacity of a potential acquisition has motivated many an acquisition. If a firm currently has earnings of $12 million that are expected to continue forever, financed entirely by common stock, a potential acquirer can apply the following logic (assuming an after-tax time value factor of 0.10 and a tax rate of 0.4):

The before-tax earnings are $20 million, and the after-tax earnings are $12 million; thus the firm is worth 12,000,000/0.10 = $120 million to the present owners. However, if the $20 million were financed completely by debt costing 0.10, then $200 million of debt could be raised. Thus, with debt financing, the assets could be acquired at a cost of $120 million, and there would be $80 million of cash left over for other uses.

Although this analysis has some deficiencies (see the cost of capital chapter), the first-order explicit effects are as indicated. The tax shelter offered by debt is real if the analysis stops at the firm level. A firm without debt or with a small amount of debt immediately becomes a merger candidate. In 1969 Congress passed a law limiting the use of debt in the type of situation described here, but this limitation is not very effective; thus the use of debt is still an attractive way of financing acquisitions.

BARGAIN PRICES AND FUNNY MONEY

The most logical reason for acquiring a firm is that the present value of the cash flows from acquisition are greater than the cost. That is, if the firm can be acquired at a "bargain" price, acquisition is desirable.

Where the common stock price of the acquiring firm is high (in the mind of the managers of the acquiring firm), it is easy to see why they would want to acquire other companies using the stock. That is, management might want to take advantage of the inflated stock prices to acquire real assets. The counterpart is also true—deflated stock prices tend to preclude the use of common stock. Until public accounting required the calculation of equivalent earnings per share, the use of convertible bonds, preferred stock, and warrants was very popular because these securities had very low explicit costs. The real costs were the dilution of the current stockholders' position, and this dilution was effectively hidden from view. The after-tax explicit cost of a 5% convertible bond was close to 2.5%, and it was not difficult to increase earnings per share by acquisitions using such securities. Accounting ignored the dilution to the stockholders' position that accompanied the issuance of the securities.

Different expectations held by the buyer and the seller can lead to an acquisition because one of the parties sees a "bargain." If the seller thinks that earnings will be a constant $10 million, but the buyer thinks earnings will grow at 0.09, the seller will capitalize the earnings at a $100 million value assuming a 0.10 time discount factor, and the buyer will see a value of $1 billion.[1]

PSYCHOLOGICAL

Growth for growth sake has undoubtedly been a factor in some mergers and acquisitions. Some managers measure their success by the size of the firm they manage, and to some extent their salaries are affected. One of the quicker ways of growing is via mergers and acquisitions; thus an impatient executive is apt to follow this path. The desire to build an empire, combined with the likely optimism associated with

[1] The seller sees $\dfrac{10,000,000}{0.10} = \$100$ million, and the buyer $\dfrac{10,000,000}{0.10 - 0.09} = $ "$1 billion".

viewing new organizational structures arising from the merger of firms, leads naturally to mergers and acquisitions.

Fear has also stimulated mergers. Some firms have sought out mergers when it appeared that they would be gobbled up by another suitor who was less desirable from the point of view of those managers controlling the firm.

REDUCTION OF RISK

Mergers and acquisitions are generally assumed to reduce risk, but this is not necessarily so. If the risk of the acquired firm is sufficiently large, it tends to contaminate the firm acquiring it.

Despite this disclaimer, certain types of mergers tend to reduce risk. Assume two firms have operations that are perfectly independent of each other, both in an economic and a statistical sense. In this situation, investors who keep their investment size the same in a merger will reduce their risk. We are assuming that a failure of one firm will not cause failure of the second firm. For example, say one group of investors owns a firm where there is .5 probability of success and .5 probability of failure, if that firm is merged with a second firm whose operations are independent, and if the original investors now own 50% of the merged firms, there will only be a .25 probability of both portions of the firms failing. Risk has been reduced (the expected return is unchanged).

THE P/E FACTOR

Some mergers have taken place because of faulty arithmetic. It has frequently been argued that a firm with a price earnings multiplier of 20 should acquire a firm with a *P/E* of 10, since the earnings once acquired would be capitalized by the market using a *P/E* of 20.

It was much more likely that the *P/E* of the merged firm would be somewhere between 10 and 20 and that the acquired firm would be capitalized at about 10 times its earnings even though it was part of a larger enterprise. For example, if the market used a *P/E* of 10 because it expected zero growth, the acquisition would slow the growth rate of the acquiring firm, and the acquisition would act as a drag.

EXAMPLE

There are two firms, and A is thinking of acquiring B. The following facts apply:

Firm	Earnings	*P/E* Multiplier	Value of Firms
A	10,000,000	20	200,000,000
B	1,000,000	9	9,000,000
	11,000,000		209,000,000

If the *P/E* of 20 applies, the new firm will be worth

$$11,000,000 \times 20 = \$220 \text{ million}$$

and A will gain $11 million by acquiring B.

Now if the *P/E* of the firm after acquisition is 19, then:

$$11,000,000 \times 19 = \$209 \text{ million}$$

and the sum of the two firms joined together is the sum of the two separate firms.

We can compute the new *P/E* by weighting the *P/E* of cash firms by the percentage of earnings it is contributing:

$$\text{Now} P/E = 20 \left(\frac{10}{11}\right) + 9 \left(\frac{1}{11}\right) = \frac{209}{11} = 19.$$

If a stagnant firm has poor reinvestment opportunities, so that it faces a low growth rate, or if the cost of stock equity is large because of a large amount of risk, the *P/E* will be relatively small. Merging this situation with a more promising situation may tend to hide the negative factors, but they will still exist.

Playing games with *P/E* factors is a dangerous type of analysis, since it bypasses all the assumptions that are implicit in a *P/E* measure (such as the level of risk, earnings opportunities, retention rate, etc.).

HOLDING COMPANIES

Holding companies had their day of glory in the 1920s in the United States, but the depression of the 1930s soured the investing community. However, one still sees several layers of companies that give the appearance of having many of the characteristics of a holding company.

The following example is meant to be illustrative of the species rather than any one company. It is artificially simplified, but it has the basic elements of a holding company. We assume there are five layers of firms, with A owning 50% of the stock of B, B owning 50% of the stock of C, and so on. In addition, we assume that each of the companies is financed with 80% debt and 20% common stock (or debt and preferred stock). The only real assets are owned by firm E, which owns $500 million of real assets. The example can easily be made more realistic by having each firm own some real assets.

	A	B	C	D	E
Assets	50,000	500,000	5,000,000	50,000,000	500,000,000
Liabilities	40,000	400,000	4,000,000	40,000,000	400,000,000
Common Stock	10,000	100,000	1,000,000	10,000,000	100,000,000

An investor who borrows $5100 from the bank could control the $500 million of assets of firm E, if he were satisfied with owning just 51% of the stock of A (he would have to borrow $10,000 to have 100% of the ownership of A).

The consolidated balance sheet is informative:

Assets	500,000,000
Debt	444,440,000
Common Stock-Minority Interests	55,550,000
Common Stock	10,000

Although this example seems to be outlandish, there are real-world counterparts. For example, at the beginning of 1971, the debt of ITT (parent) was $267 million, whereas the debt of the consolidated corporation was $1.5 billion.

A business combination takes place when there is a merger of two firms or one firm acquires a second firm. The accountant is faced with several options as to how to record the transaction, and in the past the accounting methods have greatly influenced the desirability of business combinations. Even though the accounting options have now been reduced somewhat, there are still possibilities for a firm to gain short-term advantages from the method of accounting for a merger or acquisition.

With a business combination the accountant has a series of decisions. He must first decide whether the transaction should be treated as a purchase or a pooling. If the pooling method is used, the accounting is well defined. However, if the purchase method is used, he must decide:

1. the valuation of any securities issued in the transaction to determine the total cost of the acquisition
2. the valuation of specific assets, such as marketable securities, accounts receivable, land, plant and equipment
3. the amount to be assigned to goodwill and its disposition in the future.

TELEDYNE'S ACQUISITION OF CONTINENTAL MOTORS

In 1969 there occurred a little-noticed acquisition of one corporation by another that has significant implications for investors in publicly held corporations subject to raiding. The sequence of events is illuminating as a classic of "imaginative" finance.

The 1968 annual report of Continental Motors (fiscal year ending October 31) indicated that The Ryan Aeronautical Company owned 62.2% of the outstanding shares of common stock, compared with 59.5% owned by Ryan at the end of the prior fiscal year. On December 16, 1968, Teledyne announced that 96.3% of Ryan shares had been tendered to or purchased by Teledyne, and Ryan became a Teledyne subsidiary early in 1969.

On March 19, 1969, the Board of Directors of Continental (now heavily laden with Teledyne executives) "determined that the interests of its shareholders would be best served by retaining all earnings for use in the expansion of the business," and on the common stock.

In the fourth quarter of 1968, the high of Continental stock was 33 and the low 21 3/4. In the second quarter of 1969, after the discontinuance of the dividend, the high was 24 3/4 and the low was 17 3/4. (The stock market in general was reasonably stable in this period.)

In June of 1969, the stockholders of Continental received an exchange offer. Continental Motors Corporation offered to exchange $30 principal amount of 7% subordinated debentures due in 1999 for each outstanding share of common stock. The bonds had no call protection, no conversion features, and were subordinate to other debt. The sinking fund was not to start until 1989. On May 26, 1969, the day before the first public announcement of the offer, the closing price of the common stock had dropped to $19 per share. On or about the day that stockholders received the exchange circular, triple A bonds were being sold to yield 7.8 (this is not to suggest that these subordinated debentures were triple A).

The exchange circular sent to the common stockholders stated that the retained earnings were needed for use in the firm, and no dividends would be paid "Although this policy may be reconsidered from time to time and could be changed at some time in the future . . . ." Prior to the issue of the debentures (as of April 30, 1969) the long-term debt of Continental Motors consisted of only $708,000 of notes bearing 5½% or lower interest rates. The common stockholders' equity as of the same date was $72,600,000. The debt capacity of Continental was being used to acquire Continental.

It is interesting to consider the effect an issue of $30 million of debt would have had on the earnings of Continental for the year ending October 31, 1968. The company reported earnings of $2.16 per share or $7,134,000 total.

Let us assume that $30 million of 7% debt was issued and used to retire 1,500,000 shares (purchased at a price of $20 per share) at the beginning of the year. The pro forma income statement for 1968 would be

Earnings before interest (after tax)		$7,134,000
Interest charge	$2,100,000	
Tax saving (with a tax rate of .48)	−1,008,000	1,092,000
		$6,042,000

With 1,800,000 shares now outstanding, the earnings would be $3.36 per share. Different amounts of debt would change the amounts, but not the directions of the changes that take place. The use of the debt capacity of Continental to replace common stock increases the EPS of the outstanding stock.

The debentures were listed on the New York Stock Exchange on October 2, 1969, and from that date until November 7, 1969 they traded at a high of 75 and a low of 61. On November 7, 1969, they traded at a price of 72 (the common stockholders were to receive $30 of bond per share of stock or approximately $21.60 of value in exchange for the stock).

In December 1969 Continental Motors announced a meeting that would consider and act on the merger of the company into Ryan (Ryan now being a wholly owned subsidiary of Teledyne). Since some stockholders had accepted the debenture offer, Ryan now owned 80.6% of Continental's outstanding stock. The debenture offer had served the very important purpose of increasing Ryan's ownership of Continental above two-thirds (as well as substituting debt for stock equity).

Each share of the company's stock (other than that owned by Ryan) was to be converted into securities identical to the $30 debenture already described. Thus the stockholders who originally rejected the offer of the subordinated debentures now were to be given no choice. Since Ryan owned 80.6% of the common stock, the minority stockholders could not hope to change the decision by voting (under the laws of the state of incorporation only two-thirds of the shares of common stock outstanding had to approve the merger).

The proxy statement of Continental Motors Corporation dated December 16, 1969 stated that, as of September 30, 1969, the President of Continental owned 974 shares of Teledyne and held options to purchase 1950 more shares, whereas the Chairman of the Board owned 4436 shares and held options to purchase 4432 more shares of Teledyne common. In his letter to the shareholders of Continental, the President stated "Believing it to be the best interests of the company and of all its stockholders, the Board strongly recommends the adoption of the merger proposal."

Under the law of some states, a dissenting stockholder is entitled to be paid the "fair value" of shares not voted in favor of a merger plan. A dissenting group offered to other dissatisfied stockholders an opportunity to join in a legal action. At a maximum, the fee to the lawyers representing the group was to be one-third of the value received in excess of the company's offer plus expenses. At a minimum, the lawyers were to be reimbursed for certain expenses.

After several years of litigation, the courts awarded $1.825 per share to the stockholders. The total settlement was slightly in excess of $2 million, and the legal fees and expenses were in excess of $600,000.

PURCHASE VERSUS POOLING[1]

When one firm acquires a second firm with a single firm emerging, the transaction may be accounted for using either the purchase method or pooling of interests method. We briefly describe the two methods, and then consider some pros and cons of the two methods and the criteria to be used in choosing between them.

If the pooling of interests method is used, cost based accounting is used to record the assets of the merged corporations. No goodwill is created, since the basis of the accounting is the asset values already on the books of the present firms.

Theoretically, pooling should be used when two firms merge and the surviving firm is merely an addition of the two old firms. An example of a transaction that would fit this description is a moderate-sized coal company merging with a moderate-sized steel company accomplished with an exchange of stock so that the surviving firm would be a vertically integrated firm with the both sets of stockholders owning stock in the new firm.

Unfortunately, it is impossible to describe the limiting case in which pooling would no longer be theoretically correct. Thus the decision about whether to use pooling frequently is arbitrary. Although APB 16 makes clear that for each situation either pooling or purchase is correct (not both), it is not clear how to decide which procedure is correct.

With pooling, the original costs, as recorded on the books of each company, are carried forward. This is consistent with the use of historical cost in normal going concern accounting. However, it is likely that the assets of the firm being acquired have changed drastically in value, and the acquiring firm (although the firms are being merged, it might well be that one set of management of stockholders will be in control because of size differences) although giving up stock with a value far in excess of cost, would still record the assets at cost.

---

[1]*APB Opinion No. 16: Business Combinations* offers a reasonably complete description of purchase and pooling, and defines the conditions when they can be used.

The use of cost at the time of merger will affect future expenses and incomes. The fact that future incomes are not affected adversely by a high price paid now (in the form of common stock) for the acquired firm, means that a firm can inflate its income by acquiring firms. This possibility acted as an incentive during the 1960s for mergers, since accountants were not restrictive about when a business combination could be treated as a pooling. The opportunity to use pooling led to the encouragement of mergers and acquisitions as a means of maintaining a growth pattern in earnings.

EXAMPLE

Assume firm P acquired firm S by the issuance of 1 million shares of common stock currently selling for $20 per share and that immediately before and after acquisition the balance sheets of the two companies were as follows:

| | Before | | After | |
	Firm P	Firm S	"Pooling"	"Purchase"
Assets	100,000,000	10,000,000	110,000,000	128,000,000
Liabilities	40,000,000	8,000,000	48,000,000	48,000,000
Stock equity	60,000,000	2,000,000	62,000,000	80,000,000

Assume that firm P had 6 million shares of common stock outstanding before the merger and 7 million after the merger. The market value of the stock equity of S was $20 million, and that of firm P was $120 million. Assume that the value of S's tangible assets is $10 million (there is $18 million of goodwill).

Shortly after the merger, firm P sells the assets of what was firm S (now a subsidiary) for $15 million. The income statement of P would be affected as follows:

1. With "pooling" there would be a $5 million gain, since the cost basis of the assets sold is $10 million.

2. With "purchase" there would be a $13 million loss, since the cost basis of the assets, including $18 million of goodwill, is $28 million (equal to the $20 million of common stock issued plus the $8 million of liabilities assumed).

The purchase procedure resulted in a loss of $13 million in this example, which is consistent with the sales of an asset that cost $28 million for revenue of $15 million. However, if the $18 million of goodwill had been charged to a capital account at the time of acquisition, the sale of the assets would have resulted in a gain of $5 million. Thus the immediate write-off of goodwill gives rise to a potential distortion when combined with the disposition of assets (an immediate write-off is not currently allowed unless the assets are sold).

One of the prime difficulties with purchase arises because the cost basis of the assets of the acquired company are adjusted based on the marketed transaction, but the assets of the acquiring company are not adjusted. The market value of the stock equity of P is $120 million, but the book basis is only $60 million. The records of P were not adjusted to take note of this difference, since there was not a direct transaction involving the assets of P.

Thus the purchase method moves partially away from cost-based accounting by adjusting the assets of the acquired company to take note of the new values, but the accounts of the acquiring company are left unadjusted

It is tempting to use the market transaction as the basis of adjusting P's books as well as S's assets. One difficulty would be to determine the size of the transaction necessary to trigger this adjustment. At the extreme, one could argue that any arms' length market transaction could be the basis for making the adjustment. This would lead to the use of market values of the common stock as the basis of recording the assets and stock equity of a firm.

In some situations, there is no market value for the common stock given in payment for the acquired firm. Since goodwill cannot be evaluated directly, the lack of market value would make the application of the purchase method highly subjective.

The use of pooling resulted in a gain of $5 million despite the fact that an asset costing $20 million is being sold for $15 million.

The gain results because the assets of the acquired company were not adjusted to reflect the real cost to the stockholders of the acquiring company. Since the assets are recorded at $10 million, there is a gain if they are sold for more than $10 million, despite the fact that the real cost to the stockholders of P is equal to $20 million.

Although the example illustrated an extreme situation, the immediate disposal of all the acquired assets, the same type of situation occurs if the assets are sold through time as a result of normal operations.

Conventional accounting, using historical costs, does create situations of distortion through time. However, the failings of conventional accounting are accentuated when a firm, by means of a merger, acquires assets whose market price exceeds this historical cost basis, and uses the pooling method of accounting.

Pooling is an extreme form of cost-based accounting, since it ignores the economic implications of the most immediate transaction, the merger.

CHOOSING BETWEEN THE PROCEDURES

Practitioners have established methods of determining whether pooling or purchase should be allowed as the method of recording a merger or acquisition.[2] Among the factors that have been used are the form of payment (if cash is used the transaction is considered a purchase; in the past this in turn led to part purchase, part pooling, where some cash and some stock was used, but this is not acceptable under APB 16).

For pooling of interests to be used, it is necessary that the stockholders of the acquired firm receive common stock for the largest part of their ownership interests.

APB 16 attempts to define the conditions that lead to a "purchase" and the conditions that lead to a "pooling." Unfortunately, the somewhat detailed and involved rules confuse the basic issues involving the pooling and purchase methods. APB 16 does not preclude a firm acquiring another firm whose assets are undervalued and using pooling to understate the true costs of the acquired assets (since the original costs to the seller are used as the basis of recording the assets.)

The argument that cost-based accounting is correct can be used by the advocates of pooling (use of the original costs) or the advocates of purchase (use of the costs to the corporation making the most recent purchase).

There is no question that the option of using of pooling or purchase is useful to a management wishing to shape the future earnings of its firm. However, accounting should be a means of communication and not a tool of manipulation. It is a fact that pooling encourages certain types of mergers because of the distorting effects on income (the depreciation or amortization expense is not based on the cost to the corporation that most recently acquired the assets). Pooling takes a

[2]APB 16 does not use the term "acquisition" if pooling of interests is recommended, since the word acquisition is considered to be inconsistent with the accounting practice.

primary weakness of conventional accounting (using historical costs) and magnifies it.

If one accepts the assumption that the new firm is nothing more than the combination of two firms, there is nothing logically wrong with the use of pooling, when the two firms merge. The difficulties arise because of the conventions of accounting that rely on the use of cost as the basis of accounting. Since pooling ignores the most recent market transaction (the business combination itself) and continues to use original cost, there is a likelihood of the introduction of distortions into the accounting reports. As an accounting procedure, pooling fails pragmatic tests. Too frequently it does not work as a method of recording mergers. One cannot have a firm giving $25 million of common stock for a second firm and then record the addition to assets of $4 million without there being a question about the validity of the procedure.

THE PURCHASE METHOD

If the purchase method is used, the first problem is to compute the value of the securities issued in exchange for the assets acquired. If only cash is issued, there is no measurement problem, but where securities are involved, there are some difficult problems. If there is a valid market value for the security, then that measure should be the basis of the valuation. The word, "valid" is inserted to handle the situation in which the market value is artificially set, and this situation may be expected to change in the near future.

If there is no market value, liabilities that are issued (or assumed) should be measured in terms of the present value of the contractual debt flows. Preferred stock can be valued based on the present value of the dividends promised to be paid. The market price of comparable preferred stock can be used to establish a reasonable measure of value (using the dividend yield of such stock to compute the present value of the stock is a comparable procedure.) If either the bonds or the preferred stock have conversion features, reference may be made to the market value of comparable bonds or stocks to obtain a reasonable measure of value.

In like manner, if the common stock has no market defined value, reference to comparable common stock will give a measure of value that can be used.

The utilization of face amounts or par values of the securities has no theoretical justification and should not be used. The relevant inputs for valuation are the economic characteristics of the securities.

The value of the securities issued and the liabilities assumed determines the total purchase price. This price then must be allocated to specific assets. Some of the acquired assets are relatively easily valued. For example, marketable securities and raw materials can be valued by reference to current market prices. Finished goods and work in process can also be valued working back from selling price and subtracting finishing costs and expected profits. Conceptually, plant, equipment, and land can be valued at their current replacement costs (any property to be disposed of can be valued at liquidation value).

An alternative procedure would be to start from the basic costs of the inputs and accumulate the costs, taking into consideration the extent of the completion of the products.

Some intangible assets, such as patents, may be valued individually, but basically the intangible assets are lumped together under the general title of "goodwill." Goodwill is set equal to the difference between the purchase price and the value of the specific tangible and intangible assets.

If the sum of the specifically identified tangible assets exceeds the purchase price, APB 16 recommends that the excess should be subtracted from the valuation of the long-lived tangible assets so that the sum of the tangible assets equals the purchase price.

For many years, an excess of the purchase price over the tangible asset valuation was recorded as either a direct write-off to the stock equity section, or goodwill was recorded and treated as non-amortizable asset. APB 17 recommended that such goodwill was to be written off over a period of 40 years. Not writing off the goodwill had an effect comparable to that of pooling. It gave firms an opportunity to pay large sums for other businesses, knowing that the excess of the purchase price over historical cost would not affect future incomes. This situation does not exist now if the purchase method is used.

CONCLUSIONS

Members of the accounting profession have long argued that both the pooling and purchase methods should be allowed to record business combinations. The consequences of allowing the use of pooling have not always been welcomed, but there has been a willingness to accept them. Too frequently, the choice of the method of accounting has been made based on the consequences of the method on the income measure of the firm, rather than with an aim to presenting the most useful information to present and potential investors.

Mergers and acquisitions will always be with us as one way in which a firm may grow (while the investors of the acquired firm change the nature of their investment). We may see limitations specifying what type of firms may merge, but it would be suprising to see legislation that precluded mergers and acquisitions from taking place.

The financial planner must consider the possibilities of mergers and acquisitions from two different prospectives. One is the opportunity to acquire new firms, and the other is that his firm is a possible candidate for someone else to acquire. It is extremely difficult for a manager to view a merger completely objectively. If his firm is acquiring another firm, the process is looked at as being beneficial to all parties. If his firm is being acquired, the acquiring firm is a "raider."

A firm with excess under-utilized assets and little debt that is undertaking less-than-profitable investments and has outstanding large amounts of preferred stock is a likely merger candidate. The foregoing reasons may not all be valid, but these situations do tend to attract merger-oriented firms. The financial planner should keep this in mind. Hopefully, the decisions that are made will be aimed at maximizing the well being of the stockholders.

There is another side to the merger movement. Some firms have found it profitable to divest. In May 1976 Kaiser Industries announced a plan whereby holders of the company's stock would receive shares of stock in Kaiser Aluminum, Kaiser Steel, and Kaiser Cement, which the holding company owned. The common stock price of Kaiser Industries increased by 20% on the release of this plan.

CHAPTER 14

THE CAPITAL ASSET PRICING MODEL AND INVESTMENT DECISIONS

Students learn in their first semesters
CAPM is the model for diversified investors.
Managers know what it's all about,
Nonsystematic risk has been left out.

The capital asset pricing model is an extension of the portfolio literature of the 1950s and early 1960s. The main change is that the CAP model makes use of the prices that the market is setting for return-risk trade-offs rather than using subjective measures of attitudes toward risk (such as the utility functions of investors).

We first illustrate the importance of portfolio considerations and then very briefly describe the types of calculations that can be made to evaluate real investments, applying the capital asset pricing model.

PORTFOLIO CONSIDERATIONS

Take a situation in which an investor can make a $2000 outlay and undertake an investment that promises to pay either $5000 one period from now or $0. Both the events have 0.5 probability.

Although the expected cash flows of the investments have a rate of return of 0.25, this is an extremely risky investment, and we might be reluctant to undertake an investment in which one of the outcomes is a loss of $2000, and this outcome has a 0.5 probability.

Now let us consider a second investment that also costs $2000 and promises to pay back $4000 one period from now or $0, and again both events have a 0.5 probability. The expected cash flows of this second investment have a zero rate of return, and this second investment has very little to be said in its favor (its expected present value is negative using any positive rate of interest). Thus we have two investments, one of which has a large amount of risk, and the second of which has both large risk and a zero rate of return. Taken individually, neither investment is very desirable to a person wishing to avoid risk.

Table 14.1. Outcomes of Two Investments

Event	First Investment	Second Investment	Both Investments
e_1	5000	0	5000
e_2	0	4000	4000

Table 14.1 shows the two investments, and adds some information that was not previously available. When the bad event (e_2) occurs for the first investment, the good outcome occurs for the second investment and a comparable set of outcomes occurs with the other event. The outcomes of undertaking both investments are reasonably desirable for the two possible events. For an investment of $4000, we either get back $5000 or $4000, and the rate of return of the expected cash flows is 0.125. The possibility of a large loss has been eliminated. Analyzing the portfolio of investments gives us information that was not available when we considered only the individual investments.

THE CAPITAL ASSET PRICING MODEL

The theoretical finance literature is being rewritten in terms of the capital asset pricing model. In addition, the practical men of Wall Street are applying these theories in making real decisions. The next step will be for finance officers to apply elements of the capital asset pricing model to their decisions.

The capital asset pricing model says that investors have available a market basket of risky securities and the opportunity to invest in securities with no risk of default. Risk preferences of investors dictate a combination of the market basket of the risky securities and the riskless securities. In equilibrium, the return of any security must be such that the investor expects to earn a basic return equal to the return on a default-free security plus an adjustment that is heavily influenced by the "correlation" of the security's return and the market's return.

If the return from the investment is positively correlated with the market return, the equilibrium return will be larger than the default-free return. If the correlation is negative, the equilibrium return will be smaller than the default-free return. The correlation is positive if the two returns have a positive correlation (see Figure 14.1a) and negative if they have a negative correlation (see Figure 14.1b).

We can develop a capital budgeting technique that makes use of the correlation of the investment with the market returns. If the investment is positively correlated with the market returns, there will be a subtraction from value for the risk of the investment. If the investment is perfectly independent there will be no adjustment for risk. If the investment is negatively correlated, there will be an addition to the value of the investment, since the investment tends to reduce risk. The correlation is a measure of the "systematic" risk of an investment.

If we assume that an investor is extremely well diversified and if we believe that the capital asset pricing model applies, exact formulations for the risk adjustment of an investment can be obtained. This formulation will omit the so-called "nonsystematic" risk, the risk of the firm's common stock that is independent of the market fluctuations. It is assumed that the investor is adequately diversified; thus this nonsys-

Figure 14.1a   Positive Correlation.

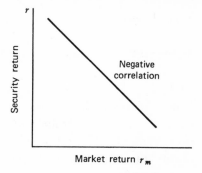

Figure 14.1b   Negative Correlation.

tematic risk does not give rise to the need for a risk adjustment.

We suggest a somewhat different approach (although the procedure is consistent with the capital asset pricing model) that is more general.

The objective of any corporate capital budgeting criterion is to select investments that will maximize the value of the common stock. With no uncertainty, we take only the time value of money into consideration. We accomplish this by application by the factor $(1 + r)^{-n}$ to future dollars to transform them back to the present.

Consider a dollar to be received in two years and a 0.10 time value factor. We can prove that the present equivalent of $1 to be received in two time periods is $0.8264 using a 0.10 time value factor. We can say that $0.8264 is the price that we would place on $1 to be received at time 2.

Now if we allow uncertainty about receiving the $1, we must take the uncertainty into consideration. Assume that the $1 is received if event e_1 takes place, and that there is a 0.8 probability of that event taking place and our receiving the $1. It is intuitively appealing to multiply the $0.8264 present value factor obtained above by 0.8 to obtain a probability adjusted time value factor of 0.6611.

Now time value and probability have been taken into consideration. However, there is a third factor to consider. Is there a risk preference? Is a dollar to be received at time 2, with the given event e_1 occurring worth more or less than $1? For example, event e_1 may be a very prosperous year and $1 is worth somewhat less than $1, because we already have many dollars. Or the event giving rise to the $1 may be a disaster (for example, the death of the bread-winner of a family) and $1, given that event e_1 has occurred, is very valuable. Thus the risk preference factor must be applied to the 0.6622 obtained above. Assume the event e_1 is a good year, and the risk preference factor is 0.95. We would then obtain a risk-adjusted present value factor of 0.6291 that would then be applied to the number of dollars to be received at time 2 with the given event for the specific investment being considered.

The 0.6291 is the product of 0.8264 and 0.8 and 0.95, which are, respectively, the time value factor, the probability of the event, and risk preference of the investor. If desired, the risk preference factor may be obtained using the capital asset pricing model, rather than subjectively as illustrated in the previous example.[1]

[1]For an expansion of this subject see H. Bierman, Jr. and S. Smidt, *The Capital Budgeting Decision*, 4th ed. Macmillan, 1975.

The object of this section is to describe an approach to capital budgeting under uncertainty that is consistent with maximizing the value of the stockholders' position. It turns out that a procedure can be developed that is very much similar to the net present value procedure except that the "present value" factors for each time period are replaced by "prices" for each event and time period that take both time value and risk into consideration.

The particular model used either makes use of the capital asset pricing model or subjective evaluations. The computations of the former model take into consideration how the cash flows of the investment vary with the overall market conditions. A difficulty with the capital asset pricing model is that a nondiversified investor may also be interested in "nonsystematic" risk, that is, the risk that the investment has independent of the market fluctuations. In a situation in which the investors of a firm are well diversified, or alternatively, the investors are willing to make investment decisions as if they were perfectly diversified, the solution techniques are extremely useful ones.

IMPLICATIONS FOR FINANCIAL PLANNING

It is easy to get lost in theory. To many readers, this chapter is an example of that situation. However, it is extremely important that you do not fail to see the import of the calculations.

Today, industry tends to use a "cost of capital" or a "hurdle rate" to implement the discounted cash flow capital budgeting techniques. Both of these measures are "averages" relecting average risks and average time value conditions and cannot be sensibly applied to unique "marginal" situations. There is no reason to think that the weighted average cost of capital can be inserted in a compound interest formula, and then be applied to a series of future cash flows to obtain a useful measure of net present value that takes both time value and risk of the investment into consideration for all investments.

When this fact was first recognized, the recommendation was made to use a default rate of interest to take time value into consideration and then adjust for risk separately. Unfortunately, exactly how to adjust for risk was not specified because we did not know how to accomplish the calculation.

Now the model described offers hope for accomplishing a systematic calculation of risk-adjusted present value. The measure reflects the investors' alternative investment return-risk trade-off opportunities or risk preferences in the same way as the rate of interest on a government bond reflects the investment opportunities when there is no default risk.

Any investment that has characteristics that differ from the average, either with respect to risk or the time shape of earnings, is apt to be very much affected by the method of valuation being suggested, compared to the conventional cost of capital calculation. Investments with low returns and desirable risk characteristics (e.g., no risk) may become acceptable, and investments with high returns but more than average risk (e.g., its returns are highly correlated with the market returns) will find it more difficult to be accepted.

Even where there is a reluctance to accept immediately the specific calculations of the type illustrated in this chapter, there will be a change in the way that management will look at alternative investments and discuss them. Initially, we can expect the capital asset pricing model or the alternative approaches to affect investment decisions in a qualitative manner. That is, after the rate of return or present value is computed, arguments will be made that will attack or advance the investment based on its risk. In the long run, we can expect the calculations illustrated (or similar calculations) to be accepted because, despite their limitations and complexity, they are the best measures that are currently available, and they are likely to be improved in the future.

One important limitation of the capital asset pricing model should be kept in mind. The model assumes that the investors are very widely diversified and equally important; it assumes that the managers of the firm are willing to make investment decisions with the objective of maximizing the well-being of this type of investor. This means that certain types of risk (for which the investor is well diversified) may be ignored in the evaluation of investments.

It is well known that objectives of firms and managers are multidimensional, and there will be a reluctance to ignore types of risk because they do not affect the well-diversified investor. Thus, even if the capital asset pricing model calculations are accepted, the analyst will still want to inject the types of considerations that are treated as being nonrelevant and that are omitted by the CAP model calculations. The so-called "nonsystematic" risk is not something that can be ignored by a management that includes among its objectives the continuity of existence of the firm. The model of this chapter readily facilitates the inclusion of these considerations.

CHAPTER 15

FINANCIAL PLANNING: PUTTING IT TOGETHER

A flexible plan is one basic ingredient
That makes business both profitable and expedient.

This book has covered a lot of ground in the areas of financial planning and has made many definite recommendations. It has offered many techniques and theories pertaining to business finance. But we will never be able to eliminate completely from consideration the easy generalization that is partially wrong. There follows a list of seven generalizations that may be classified as "myths." These myths tend to reappear in practical finance literature and business practice. The list is followed by a few comments on each myth to explain why we describe them as myths. See if you can identify the fallacy in each statement before reading the explanations.

1. The use of the present value method to evaluate investments and setting a "minimum required return" discourages growth.
2. The use of debt enables a firm to accept investments with a lower rate of return than the use of stock equity would allow.
3. If a lower dividend payout leads to a higher growth rate, the lower dividend is desirable.
4. A portion of a firm with low or zero growth should be divested by a "growth" firm.
5. A firm earning 0.10 per year on old and new investments can grow at 0.20 per year using only retained earnings.
6. The cash flows of an investment whose returns are uncertain

should be discounted at a higher rate of discount than an investment with less uncertainty.

7. A firm earning higher returns should use a higher investment discount rate (cut-off or hurdle rate) than a less profitable firm (or division).

Let us consider briefly each of the above.

1. Compared to less theoretically sound investment evaluation procedures and criteria (such as the payback method and short required payback periods), a properly applied risk-adjusted present value calculation may actually encourage investment and growth.

2. It is true that the incorporation of the debt cash flows in the present value calculations will increase the rate of return of the net of debt cash flows (the rate of return will be a return to stock equity capital), but it is far from obvious that this calculation enhances the value of an investment or makes acceptable an investment that would otherwise be unacceptable.

3. The low dividend may increase the expectation of future growth, but if the return on investment is relatively low, the stockholders might be better off with a return of capital to them and a lower corporate growth rate.

4. A perpetuity (zero growth) may have large value, as may a decaying cash flow stream; the type of generalization offered is not valid.

5. If a firm earns 0.10 on new investments and reinvests b portion of its earnings, it can expect to grow at 0.10b. If $b = 1$, and all earnings are retained, the growth rate will be 0.10, not 0.20. It is true that, in the short run, a firm can grow by being more efficient, by using resources more intensively, or by being lucky (e.g., receive a windfall price increase), but in the long run growth comes as a result of profitable investment.

6. The choice of a rate of discount and the incorporation of uncertainty into investment analysis are much more complex than is implied by a recommendation to use a higher rate of discount for more uncertainty. Generally, the compound interest formulations $(1 + r)^n$ cannot be used effectively with a risk-adjusted discount rate to evaluate real investments involving more than one time period.

7. Past profitability should not affect the investment criteria used to evaluate future alternatives. For example, a firm earning a zero return should not use a zero rate of discount to evaluate investments. The opportunity cost of the funds is relevant.

These statements are meant to be illustrative of the types of misconceptions that currently affect business decision-making. There are many more that could be listed.

While the explanations offered are somewhat incomplete, they should suggest that further study and thought are needed before generalizations such as these are applied. In business finance, relationships are frequently linked together by firm mathematical relationships, and these relationships should not be ignored.

For example, in item 5 it was claimed that a firm earning 0.10 on new investments cannot grow at 0.20 using only retained earnings. Let us consider a firm of size $1 million currently earning $100,000 per year. If the entire $100,000 is reinvested, the firm will be of size $1,100,000 and will still earn 0.10 or now $110,000, which is a growth rate of 0.10. Although a 0.10 growth rate is feasible with zero dividends, assume that the president of the firm announces a cash dividend of $50,000 and a growth rate of 0.10. What is the president assuming will happen? For the prediction to be accurate, the firm must do something different in the future than it has in the past, such as earning more than 0.10 on new investments.

Having argued against a set of generalizations, we will offer several generalizations about financial planning for your consideration. First and most important, the financial planning process must be integrated with the overall planning of the firm, and the planning taking place in other components of the firm. Financial decisions (such as the decision whether to relax or tighten credit terms) should not be made independent of the marketing strategy and the production plans for the company.

Other major economic events such as the lapsing of contracts and leases should also be noted. The full financial implications of signing any contract should be realized and such contracts carefully scrutinized. Many firms have gone bankrupt after an executive committed the firm to executing a contract when there was a small probability of a large loss, and the bad event actually occurred. The uncertainty may be in design (an exotic material is needed for an engine) or because of price changes (a contract to supply energy long-term at a fixed price signed prior to 1974 would lead to obvious financial difficulties in 1976). The corporate officers of Rolls Royce and Westinghouse understand well the possibility of these types of difficulties.

Second, the financial plans must chart the course of the firm through time. It is not unusual to find firms that know their current debt position and the debt coming due in the next 12 months, but have failed to compute the debt payments coming due over the next five years as well as the predictable major cash expenditures for that time period. One major objective of good financial planning is to have a very small probability of management being unpleasantly surprised. Surprises should be very rare and difficulties well anticipated. The classic "joke" that banks do not lend money to firms which need it ("Come back when you do not need the funds") has enough truth so that management should act so that future cash needs are anticipated.

Finally, to have successful financial planning, it is necessary to interrelate all financial decisions. Figure 15.1 shows a financial planning concept that we would recommend. All decisions are linked to all other decisions.

Consider the capital structure decision. With zero taxes and transaction costs, it can be shown that the capital structure decision is not a very important decision (investors can delever and lever firms using suitable strategies), but when we add taxes, the capital structure decision is more complex and more important. The tax deductibility of interest dictates the use of a large amount of debt. However, the fact that retained earnings are not taxed to individual investors means that common stock has an advantage compared to debt, since the investors' income tax can be deferred (assuming that investors are subject to taxation of personal income). Thus there are good tax reasons for issuing debt and good tax reasons for issuing common stock. The optimum solution will depend on the corporate and personal tax rates and provisions of the tax code as of the moment when you read this book.

Arriving at a solution to the capital structure decision will involve an assumption about the dividend policy that the firm will follow in the

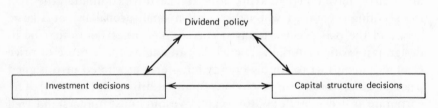

Figure 15.1   Linkage of Dividends.

future. Dividend policy and capital structure decisions cannot be solved in isolation, but rather are decisions that interact with each other. But, in addition, the investment decisions depend on the availability of cash (investible funds) and this depends on the dividend policy that is being executed. The other side of the coin is the fact that the willingness of a firm to pay dividends should depend on the availability of good investments (the presence of good investments suggests that a deferral of dividend and reinvestment of earnings is desirable). Thus the dividend, the capital structure, and the investment decisions are all linked.

Crucially important to an understanding that the financial decisions are linked is a realization that a corporation and the interests of its investors cannot be separated. The decisions being made involving dividend policy, investment decisions, and capital structure decisions can only be made after considering the interests and preferences (not always expressed or listened to) of the investors.

In the future we can expect several significant changes to take place in the management of public corporations. For one thing, labor can be expected to want to have a larger say in the type of policy decisions that are made by the board of directors. Concurrent with this event, stockholders can be expected to take a more active interest in the choice of the board of directors of a firm and the decisions made by the board. Although at present the boards are chosen by the stockholders, there are seldom any efforts to organize stockholders and influence how they vote, or to offer stockholders interesting choices. In the future we can expect to have the stockholders offered choices of candidates to the board of directors with platforms that indicate commitments to different financial strategies.

Corporations should have well-defined financial personalities so that stockholders can knowingly invest in those firms which best suit their interests. Today there is apt to be a blurring of policies, and differences are not well defined. Corporations tend to try to please broad spectrums of investors, or even all conceivable investors, with their financial decisions. It is not possible to achieve this objective, and at some stage in the future we can expect either stockholder revolts, especially as other interests become more protected, or an evolution in procedure whereby stockholders' preferences receive more consideration.

In the past, the interests of the managers and the investors have been assumed to coincide. In the future, natural differences in the objectives of the two groups can be expected to become more well defined. For example, although managers have tended to perform well in growth situations, there is evidence that they are less likely to recognize the need for contraction (giving cash back to the investors) until financial disaster strikes, and then it is likely to be too late. When a firm's common stock is selling at one times its cash flows, and the value of its plant as scrap is greater than the market value of its stock, the market is indicating a lack of faith in the ability of the management of that firm to justify its current or future investments. Combining this situation with an announcement by the firm of a massive investment project doubly compounds an unhealthy situation from the point of view of common stock investors. Although it can be argued that management knows things that the market does not know, and thus the firm should go ahead with its investment plans, it is also possible that management is excessively optimistic or serving its own interests. Market valuation of common stock of the type described indicates that a lot of people are placing bets (and money) on their judgment that the investments are not justified.

There is a time in the life of all firms when investment opportunities are not bright, and the funds should be returned to investors, just as there are times when a zero dividend is justified because of the growth possibilities arising from internal investments. There is a necessity to identify the stage of life that the firm is currently in, and execute the financial plan that is consistent with the economic realities and in the best interests of the management, workers, and investors.

The following quotation obtained in a fortune cookie in a Chinese restaurant is relevant: "Revise your plans now and guard against mistakes."

TABLES OF PRESENT VALUE

TABLE A. Present Value of $1.00

$(1+r)^{-n}$

n/r	1.0%	2.0%	3.0%	4.0%	5.0%	6%	7%	8%	9%	10%	11%	12%	13%	14%	15%
1	0.9901	0.9804	0.9709	0.9615	0.9542	0.9434	0.9346	0.9259	0.9174	0.9091	0.9009	0.8929	0.8850	0.8772	0.8696
2	0.9803	0.9612	0.9425	0.9246	0.9070	0.8900	0.8734	0.8573	0.8417	0.8264	0.8116	0.7972	0.7831	0.7695	0.7561
3	0.9706	0.9423	0.9181	0.8890	0.8638	0.8396	0.8163	0.7938	0.7722	0.7513	0.7312	0.7118	0.6931	0.6750	0.6575
4	0.9610	0.9238	0.8885	0.8548	0.8227	0.7921	0.7629	0.7350	0.7084	0.6830	0.6587	0.6355	0.6133	0.5921	0.5718
5	0.9515	0.9057	0.8626	0.8219	0.7835	0.7473	0.7130	0.6805	0.6499	0.6209	0.5935	0.5674	0.5428	0.5194	0.4792
6	0.9420	0.8880	0.8375	0.7903	0.7462	0.7050	0.6663	0.6302	0.5963	0.5645	0.5346	0.5066	0.4803	0.4356	0.4323
7	0.9327	0.8706	0.8131	0.7599	0.7107	0.6651	0.6227	0.5835	0.5470	0.5132	0.4817	0.4523	0.4251	0.3996	0.3759
8	0.9235	0.8535	0.7894	0.7307	0.6768	0.6274	0.5820	0.5403	0.5019	0.4665	0.4339	0.4039	0.3762	0.3506	0.3269
9	0.9143	0.8368	0.7664	0.7026	0.6446	0.5919	0.5439	0.5002	0.4604	0.4241	0.3909	0.3606	0.3329	0.3075	0.2843
10	0.9053	0.8203	0.7441	0.6756	0.6139	0.5584	0.5088	0.4632	0.4224	0.3855	0.3522	0.3220	0.2946	0.2697	0.2472
11	0.8963	0.8043	0.7224	0.6496	0.5847	0.5268	0.4751	0.4289	0.3875	0.3505	0.3173	0.2875	0.2607	0.2366	0.2149
12	0.8874	0.7885	0.7014	0.6246	0.5568	0.4970	0.4440	0.3971	0.3555	0.3186	0.2858	0.2567	0.2307	0.2076	0.1869
13	0.8787	0.7730	0.6810	0.6006	0.5303	0.4688	0.4150	0.3677	0.3262	0.2897	0.2575	0.2292	0.2042	0.1821	0.1625
14	0.8700	0.7579	0.6611	0.5775	0.5051	0.4223	0.3878	0.3405	0.2992	0.2633	0.2320	0.2046	0.1807	0.1597	0.1413
15	0.8613	0.7430	0.6419	0.5553	0.4810	0.4173	0.3624	0.3152	0.2745	0.2394	0.2090	0.1827	0.1599	0.1401	0.1249
16	0.8528	0.7284	0.6232	0.5339	0.4581	0.3936	0.3387	0.2919	0.2519	0.2176	0.1883	0.1631	0.1415	0.1229	0.1069
17	0.8444	0.7142	0.6050	0.5134	0.4363	0.3714	0.3166	0.2703	0.2311	0.1978	0.1696	0.1456	0.1222	0.1078	0.0929
18	0.8360	0.7002	0.5874	0.4936	0.4155	0.3503	0.2959	0.2502	0.2120	0.1799	0.1528	0.1300	0.1108	0.0946	0.0808
19	0.8277	0.6864	0.5703	0.4746	0.3957	0.3305	0.2765	0.2317	0.1945	0.1635	0.1377	0.1161	0.0981	0.0829	0.0703
20	0.8195	0.6730	0.5537	0.4564	0.3769	0.3118	0.2584	0.2145	0.1784	0.1486	0.1240	0.1037	0.0868	0.0728	0.0611
21	0.8114	0.6598	0.5375	0.4388	0.3589	0.2942	0.2415	0.1987	0.1637	0.1351	0.1117	0.0926	0.0768	0.0638	0.0531
22	0.8034	0.6468	0.5219	0.4220	0.3418	0.2775	0.2257	0.1839	0.1502	0.1228	0.1007	0.0826	0.0680	0.0560	0.0462
23	0.7954	0.6342	0.5067	0.4057	0.3256	0.2618	0.2109	0.1703	0.1378	0.1117	0.0907	0.0738	0.0601	0.0491	0.0402
24	0.7876	0.6217	0.4919	0.3901	0.3101	0.2470	0.1971	0.1577	0.1264	0.1015	0.0817	0.0659	0.0532	0.0431	0.0349
25	0.7798	0.6095	0.4776	0.3751	0.2953	0.2330	0.1842	0.1460	0.1160	0.0923	0.0736	0.0588	0.0471	0.0378	0.0304
26	0.7720	0.5976	0.4637	0.3607	0.2812	0.2198	0.1722	0.1352	0.1064	0.0839	0.0663	0.0525	0.0417	0.0331	0.0264
27	0.7644	0.5859	0.4502	0.3468	0.2678	0.2074	0.1609	0.1252	0.0976	0.0763	0.0597	0.0469	0.0369	0.0291	0.0230
28	0.7568	0.5744	0.4371	0.3335	0.2551	0.1956	0.1504	0.1159	0.0895	0.0693	0.0538	0.0419	0.0326	0.0255	0.0200
29	0.7493	0.5631	0.4243	0.3207	0.2429	0.1846	0.1406	0.1073	0.0822	0.0630	0.0485	0.0374	0.0289	0.0224	0.0174
30	0.7419	0.5521	0.4120	0.3083	0.2314	0.1741	0.1314	0.0994	0.0754	0.0573	0.0437	0.0334	0.0256	0.0196	0.0151
35	0.7059	0.5000	0.3554	0.2534	0.1813	0.1301	0.0937	0.0676	0.0490	0.0356	0.0259	0.0189	0.0139	0.0102	0.0075
40	0.6717	0.4529	0.3066	0.2083	0.1420	0.0972	0.0668	0.0460	0.0318	0.0221	0.0154	0.0107	0.0075	0.0053	0.0037
45	0.6391	0.4100	0.2644	0.1713	0.1112	0.0727	0.0476	0.0313	0.0207	0.0137	0.0091	0.0061	0.0041	0.0027	0.0019
50	0.6080	0.3715	0.2281	0.1407	0.0872	0.0543	0.0339	0.0213	0.0134	0.0085	0.0054	0.0035	0.0022	0.0014	0.0009

Table A. Present Value of $1.00 (cont'd)

n/r	16%	18%	20%	22%	24%	26%	28%	30%	32%	34%	36%	38%	40%	45%	50%
1	0.8621	0.8475	0.8333	0.8197	0.8065	0.7937	0.7813	07692	0.7576	0.7463	0.7353	0.7246	0.7143	0.6897	0.6667
2	0.7432	0.7182	0.6944	0.6719	0.6504	0.6299	0.6104	0.5917	0.5739	0.5569	0.5407	0.5251	0.5102	0.4756	0.4444
3	0.6407	0.6086	0.5787	0.5507	0.5245	0.4999	0.4768	0.4552	0.4348	0.4156	0.3975	0.3805	0.3644	0.3280	0.2963
4	0.5523	0.5158	0.4823	0.4514	0.4230	0.3968	0.3725	0.3501	0.3294	0.3102	0.2923	0.2757	0.2603	0.2262	0.1975
5	0.4761	0.4371	0.4019	0.3700	0.3411	0.3149	0.2910	0.2693	0.2495	0.2315	0.2149	0.1998	0.1889	0.1560	0.1317
6	0.4104	0.3704	0.3349	0.3033	0.2751	0.2499	0.2274	0.2072	0.1890	0.1727	0.1580	0.1448	0.1328	0.1076	0.0878
7	0.3538	0.3139	0.2791	0.2486	0.2218	0.1983	0.1776	0.1594	0.1432	0.1289	0.1162	0.1049	0.0949	0.0742	0.0585
8	0.3050	0.2660	0.2326	0.2038	0.1789	0.1574	0.1338	0.1226	0.1085	0.0962	0.0854	0.0760	0.0670	0.0512	0.0390
9	0.2630	0.2255	0.1938	0.1670	0.1443	0.1249	0.1084	0.0943	0.0822	0.0718	0.0628	0.0551	0.0484	0.0353	0.0260
10	0.2267	0.1911	0.1615	0.1369	0.1164	0.0992	0.0847	0.0725	0.0623	0.0536	0.0462	0.0399	0.0346	0.0243	0.0173
11	0.1954	0.1619	0.1346	0.1122	0.0938	0.0787	0.0662	0.0558	0.0472	0.0400	0.0340	0.0289	0.0247	0.0168	0.0116
12	0.1685	0.1372	0.1122	0.0920	0.0757	0.0625	0.0517	0.0429	0.0357	0.0298	0.0250	0.0210	0.0176	0.0116	0.0077
13	0.1452	0.1163	0.0935	0.0754	0.0610	0.0496	0.0404	0.0330	0.0271	0.0223	0.0184	0.0152	0.0126	0.0080	0.0051
14	0.1252	0.0985	0.0779	0.0618	0.0492	0.0393	0.0316	0.0253	0.0205	0.0166	0.0135	0.0110	0.0090	0.0055	0.0034
15	0.1079	0.0835	0.0649	0.0507	0.0397	0.0312	0.0247	0.0195	0.0155	0.0124	0.0099	0.0080	0.0064	0.0038	0.0023
16	0.0930	0.0708	0.0541	0.0415	0.0320	0.0248	0.0193	0.0150	0.0118	0.0093	0.0073	0.0058	0.0046	0.0026	0.0015
17	0.0802	0.0600	0.0451	0.0340	0.0258	0.0197	0.0150	0.0116	0.0089	0.0069	0.0054	0.0042	0.0033	0.0018	0.0010
18	0.0691	0.0509	0.0376	0.0279	0.0203	0.0156	0.0118	0.0089	0.0068	0.0052	0.0039	0.0030	0.0023	0.0012	0.0007
19	0.0596	0.0431	0.0313	0.0229	0.0168	0.0124	0.0092	0.0068	0.0051	0.0038	0.0029	0.0022	0.0017	0.0009	0.0006
20	0.0514	0.0365	0.0261	0.0187	0.0135	0.0098	0.0072	0.0053	0.0039	0.0029	0.0021	0.0016	0.0012	0.0006	0.0003
21	0.0443	0.0309	0.0217	0.0154	0.0109	0.0078	0.0056	0.0040	0.0029	0.0021	0.0016	0.0012	0.0009	0.0004	0.0002
22	0.0382	0.0262	0.0181	0.0126	0.0088	0.0062	0.0044	0.0031	0.0022	0.0016	0.0012	0.0008	0.0006	0.0003	0.0001
23	0.0329	0.0222	0.0151	0.0103	0.0071	0.0049	0.0034	0.0024	0.0017	0.0012	0.0008	0.0006	0.0004	0.0002	0.0001
24	0.0284	0.0188	0.0126	0.0085	0.0057	0.0039	0.0027	0.0018	0.0013	0.0009	0.0006	0.0004	0.0003	0.0001	0.0001
25	0.0245	0.0160	0.0105	0.0069	0.0046	0.0031	0.0021	0.0014	0.0010	0.0007	0.0005	0.0003	0.0002	0.0001	0.0000
26	0.0211	0.0135	0.0087	0.0057	0.0037	0.0025	0.0016	0.0011	0.0007	0.0005	0.0003	0.0002	0.0002	0.0001	
27	0.0182	0.0115	0.0073	0.0047	0.0020	0.0019	0.0018	0.0008	0.0006	0.0004	0.0002	0.0002	0.0001	0.0000	
28	0.0157	0.0097	0.0061	0.0038	0.0024	0.0015	0.0010	0.0006	0.0004	0.0003	0.0002	0.0001	0.0001		
29	0.0135	0.0082	0.0051	0.0031	0.0020	0.0012	0.0008	0.0005	0.0003	0.0002	0.0001	0.0001	0.0001		
30	0.0116	0.0070	0.0042	0.0026	0.0016	0.0010	0.0006	0.0004	0.0002	0.0002	0.0001	0.0001	0.0000		
35	0.0055	0.0030	0.0017	0.0009	0.0005	0.0003	0.0002	0.0001	0.0001	0.0000	0.0000	0.0000			
40	0.0026	0.0013	0.0007	0.0004	0.0002	0.0001	0.0001	0.0000	0.0000						
45	0.0013	0.0006	0.0003	0.0001	0.0001	0.0000	0.0000								
50	0.0006	0.0003	0.0001	0.0000	0.0000										

Table B. Present Value of $1 Received per Period

$$\frac{1-(1+r)^{-n}}{r}$$

n/r	1.0%	2.0%	3.0%	4.0%	5.0%	6%	7%	8%	9%	10%	11%	12%	13%	14%	15%
1	0.9901	0.9804	0.9709	0.9615	0.9524	0.9434	0.9346	0.9259	0.9174	0.9091	0.9009	0.8929	0.8850	0.8772	0.8696
2	1.9704	1.9416	1.9135	1.8861	1.8594	1.8334	1.8080	1.7833	1.7991	1.7355	1.7125	1.6901	1.6681	1.6467	1.6257
3	2.9410	2.8839	2.8286	2.7751	2.7232	2.6730	2.6243	2.5771	2.8113	2.4869	2.4437	2.4013	2.3612	2.3216	2.2832
4	3.9020	3.8077	3.7171	3.6299	3.5459	3.4651	3.3872	3.3121	3.2897	3.1699	3.1024	3.0373	2.9745	3.9137	2.8550
5	4.8534	4.7135	4.5797	4.4518	4.3295	4.2124	4.1002	3.9927	3.8897	3.7908	3.6959	3.6048	3.5172	3.4331	3.3522
6	5.7955	5.6014	5.4172	5.2421	5.0757	4.9173	4.7665	4.6229	4.4859	4.3553	4.2305	4.1114	3.9975	3.8887	3.7845
7	6.7282	6.4720	6.2303	6.0020	5.7864	5.5824	5.3893	5.2064	5.0010	4.8684	4.7122	4.5638	4.4226	4.2883	4.1604
8	7.6517	7.3255	7.0197	6.7327	6.4632	6.2098	5.9713	5.7466	5.5148	5.3349	5.1461	4.9676	4.7988	4.5389	4.4873
9	8.5660	8.1622	7.7861	7.4353	7.1078	6.8017	6.5152	6.2469	5.9952	5.7590	5.5370	5.3282	5.1317	4.9464	4.7716
10	9.4713	8.9826	8.5302	8.1109	7.7217	7.3601	7.0236	6.7101	6.4177	6.1446	5.8892	5.6502	5.4262	5.2161	5.0188
11	10.3676	9.7868	9.2526	8.7605	8.3064	7.8869	7.4987	7.1390	6.8051	6.4951	6.2065	5.9377	5.6869	5.4527	5.2337
12	11.2551	10.5753	9.9540	9.3851	8.8632	8.3838	7.9427	7.5361	7.1607	6.8137	6.4924	6.1944	5.9176	5.6603	5.4205
13	12.1337	11.3484	10.6350	9.9856	9.3936	8.8527	8.3577	7.9038	7.4869	7.1034	6.7499	6.4235	6.1218	5.8424	5.5831
14	13.0037	12.1062	11.2961	10.5631	9.8986	9.2950	8.7455	8.2442	7.7852	7.3667	6.9819	6.6282	6.3025	6.0021	5.7245
15	13.8650	12.8493	11.9379	11.1184	10.3797	9.7122	9.1079	8.5595	8.0607	7.6061	7.1909	6.8109	6.4624	6.1422	5.8474
16	14.7179	13.5777	12.5611	11.6523	10.8378	10.1059	9.4466	8.8514	8.3126	7.8237	7.3792	6.9740	6.6039	6.2651	5.9542
17	15.5622	14.2919	13.1661	12.1657	11.2741	10.4773	9.7632	9.1216	8.5436	8.0216	7.5488	7.1196	6.7291	6.3729	6.0472
18	16.3983	14.9920	13.7535	12.6593	11.6896	10.8276	10.0591	9.3719	8.7556	8.2014	7.7016	7.2497	6.8399	6.4674	6.1280
19	17.2260	15.6785	14.3238	13.1339	12.0853	11.1581	10.3356	9.6036	8.9501	8.3649	7.8393	7.3658	6.9380	6.5504	6.1982
20	18.0455	16.3514	14.8775	13.5903	12.4622	11.4699	10.5940	9.8181	9.1285	8.5136	7.9633	7.4694	7.0248	6.6231	6.2593
21	18.8570	17.0112	15.4150	14.0292	12.8211	11.7641	10.8355	10.0168	9.2922	8.6487	8.0751	7.5620	7.1015	6.6870	6.3125
22	19.6604	17.6580	15.9369	14.4511	13.1630	12.0416	11.0612	10.2007	9.4424	8.7715	8.1757	7.6446	7.1695	6.7429	6.3587
23	20.4558	18.2922	16.4436	14.8568	13.4886	12.3034	11.2722	10.3711	9.5802	8.8832	8.2664	7.7184	7.2297	6.7921	6.3988
24	21.2434	18.9139	16.9355	15.2470	13.7986	12.5504	11.4693	10.5283	9.7066	8.9847	8.3481	7.7843	7.2829	6.8351	6.4338
25	22.0232	19.5235	17.4131	15.6221	14.0939	12.7834	11.6536	10.6748	9.8226	9.0770	8.4217	7.8431	7.3300	6.8729	6.4641
26	22.7952	20.1210	17.8768	15.9828	14.3752	13.0032	11.8258	10.8100	9.9200	9.1609	8.4881	7.8957	7.3717	6.9061	6.4906
27	23.5596	20.7069	18.3270	16.3296	14.6430	13.2105	11.9867	10.9352	10.0266	9.2372	8.5478	7.9426	7.4086	6.9352	6.5135
28	24.3164	21.2813	18.7641	16.6631	14.8981	13.4062	12.1371	11.0511	10.1161	9.3066	8.6016	7.9844	7.4412	6.9607	6.5335
29	25.0658	21.8444	19.1884	16.9837	15.1411	13.5907	12.2777	11.1584	10.1983	9.3696	8.6501	8.0218	7.4701	6.9830	6.5509
30	25.8077	22.3965	19.6004	17.2920	15.3724	13.7648	12.4090	11.2578	10.2737	9.4269	8.6938	8.0552	7.4957	7.0027	6.5660
31	26.5423	22.9377	20.0004	17.5885	15.5928	13.9291	12.5318	11.3498	10.3428	9.4790	8.7331	8.0850	7.5183	7.0199	6.5791
32	27.2696	23.4683	20.3888	17.8735	15.8027	14.0840	12.6466	11.4350	10.4062	9.5264	8.7686	8.1116	7.5383	7.0350	6.5905
33	27.9897	23.9886	20.7658	18.1476	16.0025	14.2302	12.7538	11.5139	10.4644	9.5604	8.8005	8.1354	7.5560	7.0482	6.6005
34	28.7027	24.4986	21.1318	18.4112	16.1929	14.3681	12.8540	11.5869	10.5178	9.6086	8.8293	8.1566	7.5717	7.0599	6.6091
35	29.4086	24.9986	21.4872	18.6646	16.3742	14.4982	12.9477	11.6546	10.5668	9.6442	8.8552	8.1755	7.5856	7.0700	6.6166
40	32.8347	27.3555	23.1148	19.7928	17.1591	15.0463	13.3317	11.9246	10.7574	9.7791	8.9511	8.2438	7.6344	7.1050	6.6413
45	36.0945	29.4902	24.5187	20.7200	17.7741	15.4558	13.6055	12.1084	10.8812	9.8628	9.0079	8.2825	7.6609	7.1232	6.6543
50	39.1961	31.4236	25.7293	21.4822	18.2559	15.7619	13.8007	12.2335	10.9617	9.9148	9.0417	8.3045	7.6752	7.1327	6.5605

Table B. Present Value of $1 Received Per Period (cont'd)

n/r	16%	18%	20%	22%	24%	26%	28%	30%	32%	34%	36%	38%	40%	45%	50%
1	0.8621	9.8475	0.8333	0.8197	0.8065	0.7937	0.7813	0.7692	0.7576	0.7463	0.7353	0.7246	0.7143	0.6897	0.6667
2	1.6052	1.5656	1.5278	1.4915	1.4568	1.4235	1.3916	1.3609	1.3315	1.3032	1.2760	1.2497	1.2245	1.1653	1.1111
3	2.2459	2.1743	2.1065	2.0422	1.9813	1.9234	1.8684	1.8161	1.7663	1.7188	1.6735	1.6302	1.5889	1.4933	1.4074
4	2.7982	2.6901	2.5817	2.4936	2.4043	2.3202	2.2410	2.1662	2.0957	2.0290	1.9658	1.9060	1.8492	1.7195	1.6049
5	3.2743	3.1272	2.9906	2.8636	2.7454	2.6351	2.5320	2.4356	2.3452	2.2604	2.1807	2.1058	2.0352	1.8755	1.7366
6	3.6847	3.4976	3.3255	3.1669	3.0205	2.8850	2.7594	2.6427	2.5342	2.4331	2.3388	2.2506	2.1680	1.9831	1.8244
7	4.0386	3.8115	3.6045	3.4155	3.2423	3.0833	2.9370	2.8021	2.6775	2.5620	2.4550	2.3555	2.2628	2.0573	1.8829
8	4.3436	4.0776	3.8372	3.6193	3.4212	3.2407	3.0768	2.9247	2.7860	2.6582	2.5404	2.4315	2.3306	2.1085	1.9220
9	4.6065	4.3030	4.0310	3.7863	3.5655	3.3657	3.1842	3.0190	2.8681	2.7300	2.6033	2.4868	2.3790	2.1438	1.9480
10	4.8332	4.4941	4.1925	3.9232	3.6819	3.4648	3.2689	3.0915	2.9304	2.7836	2.6495	2.5265	2.4136	2.1681	1.9053
11	5.0286	4.6580	4.3271	4.0354	3.7757	3.5435	3.3351	3.1473	2.9776	2.8236	2.6834	2.5555	2.4383	2.1849	1.9769
12	5.1971	4.7932	4.4392	4.1274	3.8514	3.6059	3.3868	3.1903	3.0133	2.8534	2.7034	2.5764	2.4559	2.1965	1.9846
13	5.3423	4.9095	4.5327	4.2028	3.9124	3.6555	3.4272	3.2233	3.0404	2.8757	2.7268	2.5916	2.4685	2.2045	1.9897
14	5.4675	5.0081	4.6106	4.2646	3.9616	3.6949	3.4587	3.2487	3.0609	2.8923	2.7403	2.6026	2.4775	2.2100	1.9931
15	5.5765	5.0916	4.6755	4.3152	4.0013	3.7261	3.4834	3.2682	3.0764	2.9047	2.7502	2.6106	2.4839	2.2138	1.9954
16	5.6685	5.1624	4.7296	4.3567	4.0333	3.7509	3.5026	3.2832	3.0882	2.9140	2.7575	2.6164	2.4886	2.2164	1.9970
17	5.7487	5.2223	4.7746	4.3908	4.0591	3.7705	3.5177	3.2948	3.0971	2.9209	2.7629	2.6206	2.4918	2.2182	1.9980
18	5.8178	5.2732	4.8122	4.4187	4.0799	3.7861	3.5294	3.3037	3.1039	2.9260	2.7668	2.6236	2.4941	2.2195	1.9986
19	5.8775	5.3162	4.8435	4.4415	4.0967	3.7985	3.5386	3.3105	3.1000	2.9299	2.7697	2.6258	2.4958	2.2203	1.9991
20	5.9288	5.3527	4.8606	4.4603	4.1103	3.8083	3.5458	3.3158	3.1129	2.9327	2.7718	2.6274	2.4970	2.2209	1.9994
21	5.9731	5.3837	4.8913	4.4756	4.1212	3.8161	3.5514	3.3198	3.1158	2.9349	2.7734	2.6285	2.4979	2.2213	1.9996
22	6.0113	5.4099	4.9094	4.4882	4.1300	3.8223	3.5558	3.3230	3.1180	2.9365	2.7746	2.6294	2.4985	2.2216	1.9997
23	6.0442	5.4321	4.9245	4.4985	4.1371	3.8273	3.5592	3.3253	3.1197	2.9377	2.7754	2.6300	2.4989	2.2218	1.9998
24	6.0726	5.4609	4.9571	4.5070	4.1428	3.8312	3.5619	3.3272	3.1210	2.9386	2.7760	26304	2.4992	2.2219	1.9999
25	6.0971	5.4669	4.9476	4.5139	4.1474	3.8342	3.5640	3.3286	3.1220	2.9392	2.7765	2.6307	2.2994	2.2220	1.9999
26	6.1182	5.4804	4.9563	4.5196	4.1511	3.8367	3.5656	3.3297	3.1227	2.9397	2.7768	2.6310	2.4996	2.2221	1.9999
27	6.1364	5.4919	4.9636	4.5243	4.1542	3.8387	3.5669	3.3305	3.1233	2.9401	2.7771	2.6311	2.4997	2.2221	2.0000
28	6.1520	6.5016	4.9697	4.5281	4.1566	3.8402	3.5679	3.3312	3.1237	2.9404	2.7773	2.6313	2.4998	2.2222	2.0000
29	6.1656	5.5093	4.9747	4.5312	4.1585	3.8414	3.5687	3.3316	3.1240	2.9406	2.7774	2.6313	2.4999	2.2222	2.0000
30	6.1772	5.5168	4.9789	4.5338	4.1601	3.8424	3.5693	3.3321	3.1242	2.9407	2.7775	2.6314	2.4999	2.2222	2.0000
31	6.1872	5.5227	4.9824	4.5359	4.1614	3.8432	3.5697	3.3324	3.1244	2.9408	2.7776	2.63152.40999		2.2222	2.0000
32	6.1959	5.5277	4.9854	4.5376	4.1624	3.8438	3.5701	3.3326	3.1246	2.9409	2.7776	2.6315	2.4999	2.2222	2.0000
33	6.2034	5.5320	4.9878	4.5390	4.1632	3.8443	3.5704	3.3328	3.1247	2.9410	2.7777	2.6315	2.5000	2.2222	2.0000
34	6.2098	5.5356	4.9898	4.5402	4.1639	3.8447	3.5706	3.3329	3.1248	2.9410	2.7777	2.6315	2.5000	2.2222	2.0000
35	6.2166	5.5386	4.9915	4.5411	4.1644	3.8450	3.5708	3.3330	3.1248	2.9411	2.7777	2.6215	2.5000	2.2222	2.0000
40	6.2335	5.5482	4.9966	4.5439	4.1659	3.8458	3.6712	3.3332	3.1250	2.9412	2.7778	2.6316	2.5000	2.2222	2.0000
45	6.2421	5.5523	4.9986	4.5449	4.1664	3.8460	3.5714	3.3333	3.1250	2.9412	2.7778	2.6316	2.5000	2.2222	2.0000
50	6.2463	5.5541	4.9995	4.5452	4.1666	3.8461	3.5714	3.3333	3.1260	2.9412	2.7778	2.6316	2.5000	2.2222	2.0000

INDEX